Book Launch November 2014

Comments posted on Amazon from readers about *We Fought to Win: American World War II Veterans Share Their Stories*:

"My dad was a navigator in WW II, so I was anxious to read this book. Once I started reading, I couldn't put it down." Doreen A.

**

"Fascinating stories. Lessons from history. Miraculous survivals. This book has them all, including four women -- Army nurse, Women's Army Auxiliary Corps (WAAC) and two who served as Women Airforce Service Pilots (WASP)." Shirley B.

**

"In every story, Reusser captures the emotions and feelings of the veterans and what he/she experienced. A great read that truly displays the courage and sacrifice of the men and women from northeast Indiana who helped fight and win World War II." Justin K.

**

"This book brings the reality of these men and women to life. It is important to capture the memories of these brave people who served in World War II before they can no longer share their stories. I plan to use the stories and images with my first grade class." Julia J.

**

"I bought this book for my father, who grew up during World War II. He and my mother both enjoyed it so much that they kept snitching it from each other. They enjoyed it greatly." Debbie W.

**

Each story includes a current photo of the vet and war time pictures. It is often difficult to get war veterans to discuss those combat days, but this book reveals what many experienced. A must nonfiction book for any War book collection. Alan D.

**

"We read about battles in history books, but those books don't share the personal experiences of those serving on the front lines. The stories are a nice length, and it is easy to start and stop reading the book as necessary." Cheryl G.

Comments posted on Amazon from readers about *They Did It for Honor: Stories of American WWII Veterans:*

"The book is well written in a manner that flows quickly and appeals to a wide range: teens can understand it, seasoned military vets will appreciate it. Accounts are shared about various locations, theaters of operation, and branches of the service. Lots of pictures, both from archives and from the veterans themselves, add much interest and great perspective." Debra A.

**

"While reading this book, you'll feel you are right there in the foxhole or aboard a sub, or freezing on the battle front, or liberating a Jewish prison camp. I guarantee you will feel proud of those who served." Harold Wolf

**

"The information shared here from the hearts of 34 World War Two Veterans is simply stunning. It will touch the hearts of readers and bring insights to the World War Two era in a way few have ever accomplished." Curtis R.

**

"Working in library service, I can say this book has been a great addition to our library's adult and local history collections. I would highly recommend it to other libraries and as a resource for teachers to create a living picture of American history and sacrifice." Shana N.

"As a social studies teacher, I find this book has helped to provide a local connection and stories to reference when teaching about the war." Bryan L.

We Fought to Win: American World War II Veterans Share Their Stories

WWII Legacies Series

Book 1

Kayleen Reusser

Kayleen Reusser Media

We Fought to Win: American World War II

Veterans Share Their Stories

Published in the United States by

Kayleen Reusser Media

Printed in the United States of America

Cover illustration by Kayleen Reusser. Additional photos used with permission of the
U.S. Navy, U.S. Army, veterans from the book.

First edition published 2014 by Oak Creek Publishing under the title: WWII
Legacies: Stories of Northeast Indiana Veterans

The information provided within this book is for general information
purposes only. While the author has tried to provide correct information,
there are no representations or warranties, express or implied, about the
completeness, accuracy, reliability, suitability or availability with respect to
the information, products, services or related graphics contained in this
book for any purpose. Any use of this information is at one's own risk.

Table of Contents

Acknowledgements

Thanks to my supporters, especially members of the Bluffton Christian Writing Club and Ft Wayne Christian Writing Club for encouraging me with kind and helpful words in the writing of this book.

My husband John and children -- Lindsay, Amanda, Christopher – have put up with my writing career for decades. You're the best. I'll love you forever.

Introduction

My interest in writing this book began a few years ago when I interviewed World War II veterans as profiles for a weekly newspaper column. I quickly gained an appreciation of what it was like to have been involved in what was truly a world war more than seven decades ago. I did not grow up surrounded by military stories. My dad was deferred to farm and raise food for people at home and soldiers abroad. My father-in-law was deferred for the same reason. Feeding our country was a huge responsibility and I'm proud of them.

But my husband John retired from the Air Force and our son is an Air Force pilot, having served in Afghanistan. I can't imagine sending more than one son to war and yet I've talked to veterans who had as many as four family members serving. They usually did not know where the others were or what was happening until the end of the war. Today various forms of communciation keeps us close to loved ones overseas. Back then, scuttlebutt often carried news.

The idea to put some of those amazing stories into a book took hold. I expanded the area to include male and female veterans who live in Adams, Allen, Huntington, Whitley and Wells counties. These stories of people who served in the Army, Marines, Navy and Army Air Corps include experiences in D-Day, Battle of Attu, Iwo Jima, Battle of the Bulge, Remagen and Operation Market Garden, among others.

The challenge in writing these stories was in tapping memories of events from long ago, sometimes for the first time. I never pressured for details, simply accepted whatever they could recall, then pieced them together as coherently as possible. We talked, laughed and even cried together. Much information will not make it into print due to confidentiality. Certain pieces of information I tried to include in each story were year of birth, date of enlistment/ draft; unit within branches; date of separation or discharge.

Without exception the veterans told me they did not want to be called heroes. "We only did what we had been trained to do. The men and women who died during the war were the heroes," they said. I respect that. But I believe each person serving at home or abroad who has ever done what they were told to protect our country was, and is, a hero. By writing this book I hope to create an appreciation of what this generation experienced for our benefit. Their unique and precious stories are lessons for every generation. May we never take our freedoms for granted.

Bob Batchelder – Army / Europe

Robert 'Bob' Batchelder of Fort Wayne landed on Omaha Beach at Normandy on June 6, 1944, as part of the D-Day invasion. "I crawled down the side of our landing craft with medical supplies into the cold water while guns strafed the water around us," he said. "Thankfully, I knew how to swim."

He was a member of the 457th Medical Collecting Company. "We collected injured and dead bodies on the battlefield." Batchelder's division supported the 82nd airborne division. The 82nd's most ambitious operation of the war to that point was the airborne assault phase of Operation Overlord, or D-Day.

On June 5 and 6 and days following, paratroopers, parachute artillery elements, and other troops boarded hundreds of transport planes and gliders (engineless aircraft towed into the air to their target by military transport planes) for the assault on the shores of Normandy France.

German troops hid in casemates and hedgerows eight feet thick. Casemates were fortified gun structures from which guns were fired. Hedgerows were maze-like structures that housed machine guns and other firepower. For five days, Batchelder and other medical personnel treated casualties in a 12-foot-by-20-foot tent for a temporary field hospital. "We used morphine as penicillin was not yet readily available," he said.

Batchelder, who attended Central Catholic High School in Fort Wayne, had been drafted in the fall of 1942. He was sent to Camp Perry in Ohio for basic training. Batchelder's three brothers were also soldiers in the war.

> *"We slept in foxholes in freezing weather and lots of snow. We lost more troops to frostbite and gangrene than gun shots."*

At Camp Maxey, north of Paris, Texas, Batchelder and other GI's were tested to determine skills and aptitude. Batchelder, who had been employed in the wholesale tobacco business, was shocked to learn he tested high for medical terminology and procedures.

Batchelder had wanted to join the Army Air Corps. Instead, he was assigned as a medic with the 457th Army Medical Collecting Company. "We trained for 13 weeks to learn how to adapt to working near the front line," he said. "As litter bearers, we got injured bodies off of the field of battle as quickly and safely as possible."

During winter 1944-1945, Batchelder fought in another momentous conflict -- Battle of the Bulge in the Ardennes Forest of Belgium. "It was a horrendous experience," he said. "We slept in foxholes in freezing weather and lots of snow. We lost more troops to frostbite and gangrene than gun shots."

The troops endured for six days with no air support until the clouds finally broke and Allied fighters and bombers arrived. By the end of the battle in February, approximately 89,000 soldiers had been wounded and 19,000 killed, making the Battle of the Bulge one of the largest and bloodiest battles fought by the U.S. during the war.

Not everything was a gruesome task for Batchelder. In May 1945 he was standing guard duty outside a tent in an Allied camp in Germany when a German male civilian approached him. The German spoke English to Batchelder: "I would like to surrender."

Batchelder took the civilian to his commanding officer in the officer's tent, and then resumed his post. Batchelder found out later the man was Wernher von Braun, Germany's top rocket scientist. "He wanted to leave Germany because he didn't want to give information about the V-2 missile to Hitler," said Batchelder. The V-2 rocket was a short-range ballistic missile developed in Germany. It was designed to target London. Von Braun was smuggled out of Germany to England and then to the U.S.

Batchelder's war experiences continued until he was discharged in January 1946. He had spent a year and a half overseas, fighting his way through Germany, England, France, Belgium, Holland and Luxembourg. He was never injured. All of Batchelder's brothers returned home safely from the war. After the war, Batchelder worked in the wholesale candy business until retiring in 1985. He and his wife Edna Sell married in 1947. They were parents to one son. He and Edna are both deceased. "It was a difficult time but I was glad to serve my country in World War II," he said.

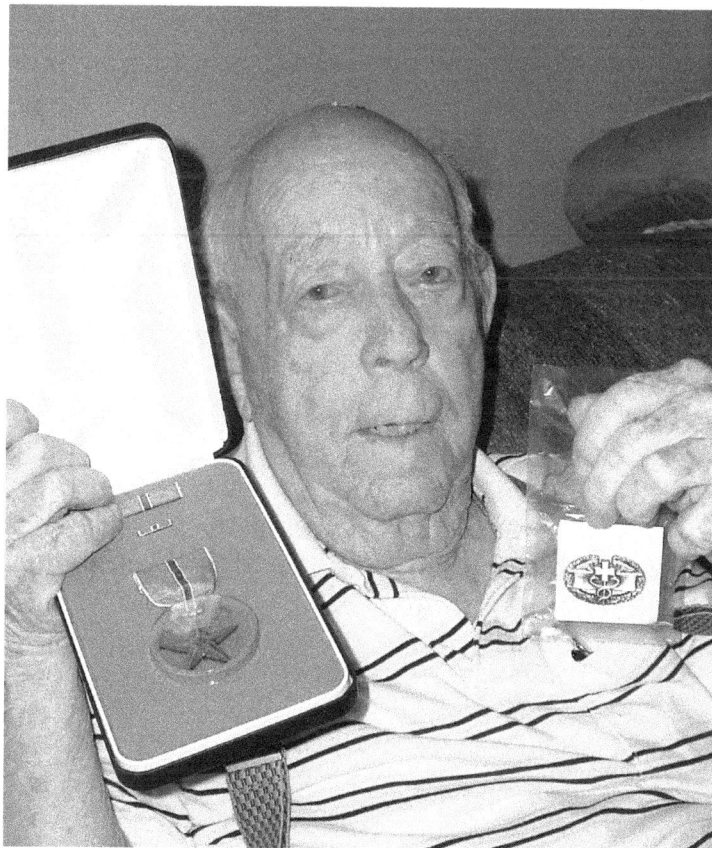

On June 6, 1944, Gen. Dwight D. Eisenhower gives the order of the day -- 'Full victory-nothing else' -- to paratroopers in England, just before they participate in the invasion of Europe.

Homer Bates — Army Air Corps / Pacific

Being awarded a Distinguished Flying Cross medal and meeting an American president are a few of the highlights of Homer Bates' military service during World War II. Born in 1923, Bates moved to Wells County where he graduated from East Union Center High School in Wells County in 1941. In December 1942 he enlisted in the Army Air Corps (the name would later be changed to Air Force). After testing high for skills needed to work with aircraft, Bates was sent for technical training as an aerial gunner to schools in North Carolina, Illinois and Colorado.

Bates was assigned to the 20th Air Force 58th Bomber Wing and assigned a gun turret on a B-29. As the B-29s were still in production, he and other gunners practiced on B-17 simulators since they had similar controls. When it came time to practice shooting, the gunners experienced a problem.

"Several of us were told to shoot painted ammo (ammunition) simultaneously at a banner flying behind a tow plane," he said. "It served as a moving target and we were judged on our shooting abilities. At first the judges could not tell whose shots went where. So we were given ammo painted different colors. The judges could then tell by colors of holes which gunners needed more practice."

His first mission over Japan took place June 1944. "For more than a year it was a steady routine of dropping bombs and encountering enemy fighters and heavy accurate flak," he said. His longest mission to Nagoya lasted 18 hours. During the war, Bates flew 33 missions over Japan in B-29s.

In February 1944 Bates' crew was ordered to fly a B-29 Typhoon McGoon III to Washington D.C. No reason was given for the special trip. Upon landing at Bolling Field, the crew commander was met by General Hap Arnold and his staff. Each of the crew members was greeted and asked to explain the aircraft so he could brief the president. The following morning the crew was completing their pre-flight check of equipment when they saw a limousine pull up beside the plane, along with an official-looking motorcade. President Franklin D. Roosevelt had arrived.

He and members of his family began questioning the crew about the aircraft. Anna Roosevelt Boettiger and her two teenaged children, Eleanor and Curtis, went into the nose section and asked questions of the crew. "It was obvious she was well versed about the plane," said Bates.

> *A limousine pulled up beside the plane, along with an official-looking motorcade. President Franklin D. Roosevelt had arrived.*

The president remained in the vehicle but appeared pleased with the aircraft. "That was perhaps the only time the President ever saw a B-29," said Bates. Considering that the B-29 project cost $3 billion and the A-bomb cost $2 billion, the president's approval was a relief to the crew. The president ended the session by shaking hands with each crew member.

Staff Sgt. Bates was discharged November 2, 1945. For his bravery and contribution to the war effort he was awarded the Distinguished Flying Cross and several other medals. Military life had gotten into Bates' blood. He joined the Indiana Air National

Guard from 1954-1961. He re-joined the Air Force and spent a year in France during the Berlin Wall Crisis, then re-joined the Indiana Air National Guard full time until 1982, retiring as a Master Sergeant.

Bates and Helen Roudebush married in 1950 and became parents to six children. In 2015 Bates, accompanied by a daughter and friend, attended a military reunion in which he fulfilled a goal—to crawl through the 33-foot tunnel that connected front and back sections of a B-29 bomber above the bomb bays.

At age 91, Bates received permission from the director of the New England Air Museum in Windsor, Conn., where the reunion was being held to accomplish his dream. The permission came with one condition. "My daughter had to go along with me," he said.

Near the end, Bates, tiring, was pulled from the tunnel by helpful hands. He emerged smiling.

Bates has participated in Honor Flight for Northeast Indiana. "I wouldn't change anything about my military service," he said.

Homer Bates (seated, second from left) and members of his military group meet for a reunion in 2015.

Richard Beitler – Army / Pacific

On Leyte Island in the Philippines American soldiers reconnoitered in the Bataan Mountains. It was January 1945 and American forces were trying to recapture the Bataan peninsula from the Japanese. All was quiet until the third night. When the enemy began firing, part of Richard Beitler's company went to high ground to fight. Beitler from Berne, Ind., stayed in the valley with other soldiers, firing all night. Many Americans were killed in what would be later called the Battle of Zig Zag Pass.

Beitler, a 1935 graduate of Berne High School, had worked six years at Dunbar Furniture in Berne before being drafted in the U.S. Army. In September 1941 Beitler completed basic training at Camp Shelby, Miss. The following year he participated in amphibian training in Florida and maneuvers in western Louisiana. In 1943 he received instruction at Camp Livingston in northern Louisiana.

When Beitler shipped out on January 1, 1944, he was a member of Company G, 152nd Infantry, 2nd Battalion, 38th Division out of Newcastle, Ind. The troops sailed on a former cruise ship, the SS Lurline in a 30-ship convoy.

When Beitler's ship left the convoy, it zigzagged alone for two weeks to Hawaii. "The movements were to confuse enemy subs on their radar," he said.

Beitler's company trained for combat five months in Hawaii. They then headed toward Oro Bay in New Guinea on a liberty ship. "It was a 21-day trip, but I was never seasick," he said. During their four months in Oro Bay, the soldiers trained by day and unloaded ships at night.

The Battle of Zig Zag Pass was ferocious with American troops engaged in heavy conflict in the hills along the western side of the Philippines. One captain and five lieutenants led the company into battle. By the time the Japanese retreated weeks later, only one captain and lieutenant were still alive.

The lieutenant suffered shell-shock (today referred to as post-traumatic stress syndrome). When the captain commissioned four platoon sergeants as second lieutenants, Beitler was subsequently promoted to platoon sergeant.

> ***When a Japanese bullet struck Beitler's helmet during the battle at Zig Zag Pass, it drilled a hole, grazing his scalp.***

Beitler had attended church regularly while growing up. He prayed often as a soldier and carried a New Testament with him into battle. Once, when a Japanese bullet struck his helmet during battle at Zig Zag Pass, it drilled a hole, grazing his scalp. Beitler, not seriously wounded, suffered only at being told he could not keep the helmet. "It would have been a good souvenir," he said.

By summer 1945, Beitler and other American troops were told to prepare for what they believed would be the biggest conflict of the war – invasion of the Japanese mainland. To the relief of the soldiers, the invasion was cancelled following the bombing of Nagasaki and Hiroshima. When the Japanese emperor surrendered in Tokyo Harbor on September 2, 1945, the war was over!

After four years in service, Tech Sgt. Beitler had earned the required number of points to be shipped home. He left the Philippines in September 1945 and arrived at Camp Atterbury a month later where he was officially discharged. Beitler's four brothers had also fought in the war and arrived home safely.

Back in Berne, Richard Beitler married Margaret Sprunger in 1948. They became parents to six children. Margaret died in 2011. Beitler worked at Dunbar Furniture until he retired in 1985. For many years Beitler attended reunions for Company G until they were disbanded. In 2013 he participated in Honor Flight of Northeast Indiana.

Beitler believes in God's provision during his time as a soldier. "I had several close calls while overseas," he said. "I prayed often and read my New Testament. I valued the words of Psalm 121, verse 8: 'The Lord will watch over your coming and going both now and forevermore.' I believe God saw me through those tough times."

U.S. Marines and their dogs scout through the jungle at Bougainville on New Guinea, ca. December 1943.

George Edward Buhler — Army / Europe

In 1941, George Buhler was 22 years old when he was drafted into the United States Army. A native of Passaic, New Jersey, he reported to Fort Dix near Trenton for basic training. Since it was early in the war, the Army accommodated troops in tents because there were not enough barracks. "We trained in World War I uniforms and used broomsticks because there were no supplies," he said.

Having ridden a motorcycle as a civilian, Buhler was assigned duties of a military policeman. He was issued a 45-cubic-inch, 2-cylinder Harley motorcycle, .45 pistol and Brownie automatic machine gun.

Buhler received training in maneuvers in Fort Jackson in South Carolina; Yuma, Arizona; Needles, California and Fort Benning in Georgia. Finally, in December 1943 as a member of the 1st Army, 8th Infantry division, he climbed aboard a ship at New York City to head for Ireland. "We traveled in a convoy of ships filled with American troops," he said.

Troops trained for three months, then in early June 1944 prepared to cross the English Channel. Buhler's squadron boarded an LST (Landing ship, tank) to land on the beaches of Normandy, France.

"We were the 18th group to hit the beach since the invasion began on June 6," said Buhler.

"Normandy was brutal. We were all so scared and numb, but we knew it had to be done."

His group was directed toward Utah Beach where German troops waited with artillery behind cement compounds called pillboxes. Many Allies were shot in the water and on the shore. "It was brutal," he said. "We were all so scared and numb, but we knew it had to be done." According to research done by the United States National D-Day Memorial Foundation, Allied personnel killed during the D-Day invasion numbered approximately 4,400.

In summer 1944 Buhler's division moved to Brest, Germany, a major submarine port Allied forces hoped to seize. Securing it from the Germans had proved difficult. Now British troops dropped 2,000-pound bombs. "We stayed in foxholes much of the time to avoid concussion from the explosions," said Buhler. By September 1944 the Allies had recaptured the town.

In September Buhler was part of the Allied liberation of Paris. He performed traffic duty at the Champs Élysées. That fall Buhler's division encountered further ferocious combat in Germany's Hertgen Forest, east of the Belgian–German border. "It was cold and brutal," he said. "Mud came up to our knees." Casualties in the Hertgen Forest were said to number in the tens of thousands.

Buhler traveled to the Battle of the Bulge in Belgium's Ardennes Forest. "We lost a lot of people there," he said. "There was a lot of misery." Sleeping outside for weeks in foxholes in record-low temperatures caused frostbite for many GI's.

In March 1945 Buhler was involved with the taking of the railroad bridge at Remagen, Germany. Aware that the Rhine River posed the last major geographic obstacle to Allied troops, Hitler had ordered the bridge over the river destroyed. "The

Germans shot 18-inch shells from railroad cars at us," he said. Allied troops saved the bridge, enabling 8,000 troops to cross it.

Buhler's brothers – Arthur, Eugene and Fred – were also drafted into the United States military. Sadly, Eugene was captured when his B-17 bomber was shot down by the Germans. "All our family knew was that Eugene had been imprisoned," he said. George, Arthur, and Fred looked for Eugene in every German concentration camp they helped the Allies to liberate. Thankfully, Eugene was among the 250,000 prisoners of war liberated at the war's end in May 1945. Weighing 80 pounds after being fed rotten potatoes and cabbage for months, Eugene's family feared for his life. Medical care and treatment saved him.

On September 15, 1945, George Buhler was discharged. All four Buhler brothers returned to their family home in New Jersey following the war's end. In 1947 George married and he and his wife Rose became parents to two children. George worked in maintenance positions throughout his life until retirement. The Buhlers live in Berne.

"The war was such a loss to the world," he said. "So many men and women of all nationalities lost their lives for the desire of one mad man to rule all."

American troops of the 28th Infantry Division march down the Champs Elysees, Paris, in a Victory Parade, August 1944.

Eugene Dettmer – Army / Europe

"I saw men who had been blown up," said Fort Wayne native Eugene Dettmer. "If I had been on the first wave that landed on Utah Beach, I would have been killed." Dettmer was part of the landing of Allied soldiers on the three-mile stretch of French land that comprised the westernmost flank of Normandy on June 6, 1944.

Dettmer was in the 468th AAA Battery C attached to the Third Army. He was assigned to drive jeeps for officers and half-track 468s, which were armored anti-aircraft vehicles used heavily by U.S. troops during the war. "Dad had taught me basic auto mechanics so that gave me skills," he said.

Fighting with an artillery unit in war was heady stuff for Dettmer. Born in Fort Wayne, his family moved to the town of Tocsin in northern Wells County where he grew up.

Dettmer planned to graduate from Ossian High School in May 1943, but the Army had other plans for him. Dettmer, who turned age 18 in January 1943, was drafted into the Army, following his junior year at Ossian High School. While his classmates completed their senior year, Dettmer finished basic training at Fort Eustis, Virginia. More training followed at Fort Miles Standish in Taunton, Mass.

In March 1944 Dettmer and thousands of other young American soldiers disembarked by ship for England. They moved through Scotland to France, being told along the way to prepare for battle. Little could they imagine they would be involved in one of the deadliest battles in the history of the world.

> *"Our timing for D-Day was off by one day. That may have confused the Germans, but they put a good fight."*

Dettmer was one of 20,000 soldiers who landed on Utah Beach on June 18, 1944. An estimated 1,700 motorized vehicles, including half-tracks, were used to fight that day. P-51 and P-47 aircraft seized beach exits, captured key transportation and communication points and blocked German counterattacks. C-47 planes carried wounded soldiers to safety.

American troops were not the only soldiers at Normandy. "British forces shot cannons and pilots helped with airborne assault," said Dettmer.

Although surrounded by violence and destruction, Allied casualties numbered fewer than those on nearby Omaha Beach. "Our timing was off by a day due to weather," said Dettmer. "That may have confused the Germans, but they still put a good fight."

After securing the beaches of Normandy, Dettmer and other troops pushed through Luxembourg toward Berchtesgaden in southern Germany, near Austria's border. The Nazis had purchased sections of the area in the 1920s as its headquarters. Nicknamed 'Eagles Nest' for its lofty perch and known as one of Hitler's residences, it was a prime target for Allied forces.

By April 1945 Allied forces had secured the region (Hitler was not present during the takeover). American soldiers used the place as a resort. "We each had our own room to sleep in," said Dettmer.

The scenery captured the attention of the soldiers who now had time on their hands. "Lake Königssee was beautiful," he said.

The Allies stayed at Berchtesgaden until the war ended in September 1945 with the surrender of Germany and Japan and several months beyond, maintaining peace.

After serving 21 months overseas, Corp. Dettmer was issued orders to go home so he left Europe to return to the U.S. He arrived in Tocsin at his family's home on December 29, 1945, too late for Christmas but joyous. He credits religious faith for his safety. "God placed me with an anti-aircraft regiment to protect me," he said.

Dettmer received five battle stars for his involvement with Utah Beach. He also received the standard $300 which the government issued to every GI at discharge.

After marrying his childhood sweetheart, Jacqueline Lindemann, in 1946, Dettmer worked for Stucky's appliances in Fort Wayne for 43 years. The couple became parents of three children.

In 1970, Dettmer completed his high school education at Central High School (now Anthis Career Center). Although he didn't receive a diploma from Ossian High School, he was included as a member of the class of 1944.

Dettmer participated in the Honor Flight for Northeast Indiana on May 8, 2013. "It was truly amazing how we were treated by the volunteers and people who waved flags and helped us," he said. "The war memorials, Lincoln Memorial and Arlington Cemetery were great sights to see and ones which everyone should see in one's lifetime. I had a great time."

The lovely medieval German village of Berchtesgaden was the hometown for Germany's chancellor, Adolph Hitler, and many of his military advisors during World War II. Photo taken by author.

Bob Foster – Army / Europe

Bob Foster of Fort Wayne was one of thousands of Allied troops who arrived at Normandy, France, in mid-June 1944 for the Battle of Cherbourg. This skirmish followed the successful Allied landings on June 6.

Foster and other Allied troops disembarked from landing ship tanks (LSTs) by descending 20-foot ladders into cold water before scrambling toward shore. Taught how to shoot during basic training, the troops' marksmanship skills were of little help as they became easy targets for German marksmen on shore. "I lost a friend during that invasion," said Foster.

A 1940 graduate of Bluffton High School, Foster had been raised by a father who served in the French Signal Corps during WWI. It didn't surprise the family when Bob enlisted in the Army in October 1943. "I just had to go and fight," he told Phyllis Elzey whom he had married in 1941. After a physical exam at Fort Benjamin Harrison in Indianapolis, Foster completed basic training at Aberdeen Proving Ground in Maryland. Foster was assigned to the 84th Infantry Division Railsplitters, Company A, 333rd Regiment where he trained as a tank mechanic.

For those who made it to shore at Cherbourg, the fighting continued for two weeks with an Allied victory. Six months later, Foster was involved in another brutal conflict at the Battle of the Bulge.

> *During the Battle of the Bulge, soldiers fought in foxholes filled with snow. Many soldiers froze to death. Dead soldiers were stacked 20 feet high.*

The conflict which began on December 16, 1944, took place during one of the coldest winters on record. For three months the soldiers fought in foxholes filled with snow. Many soldiers froze to death. "Dead soldiers were stacked 20 feet high," said Foster.

Struggles against the elements were only part of the challenge to survive. When Foster's captain put him in charge of the platoon for a raid on a town in Belgium, he handed Foster a Browning Automatic Rifle (BAR) with 15 clips of 30-caliber shells, weighing approximately 15 pounds. "Our other BAR man had been killed," said Foster. The BAR could shoot like a machine gun, but was little protection against German tanks which shot 88-millimeter shells, the biggest in the world.

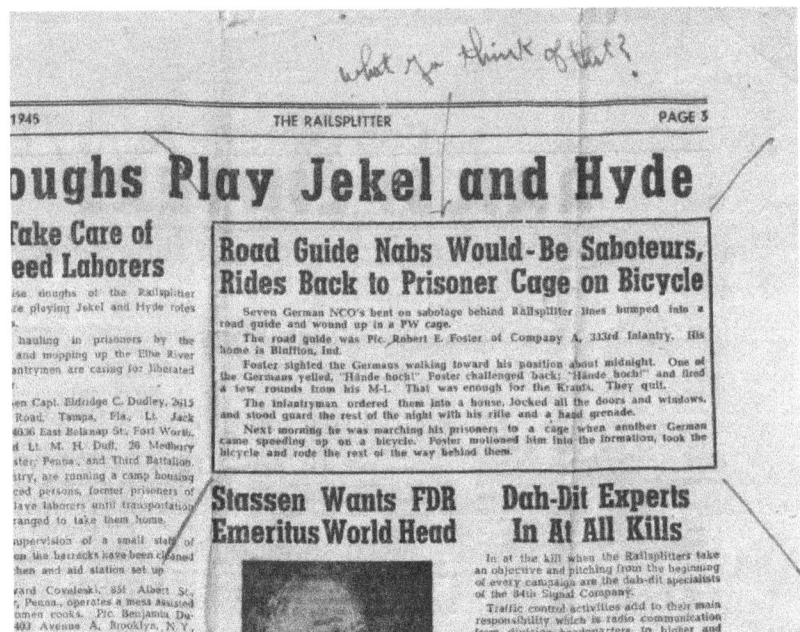

When the Germans opened fire on Foster's platoon, a shell critically damaged his captain's leg. Foster was also injured in the knee and head but tried to help his captain, pressing his hand against the wound to staunch the flow. Sadly, the captain died. Foster, weak from his own blood loss, collapsed. Medics rushed him to an aid station. Later, he was transferred to hospitals in Paris and England where he recovered and was returned to his unit in Germany. Foster's adventures continued.

One night near Bielefeld he was leading sentry patrol when he heard footsteps on a nearby wooden bridge. He and his patrol hid in bushes, waiting for the right moment before jumping five German soldiers, taking them as POWs.

Foster's company was decorated for bravery on June 26, 1945, by President Harry Truman, General Dwight D. Eisenhower and Field Marshall Bernard Montgomery. Foster was presented with a Bronze star by Truman who shook his hand.

During the war, Foster and his wife wrote letters to each other. She reminded him of his spiritual heritage and Bob believed he saw evidence of God's care for him through the difficult times. One cold, rainy night as American soldiers sought refuge in foxholes outside a German village, a German Lutheran military chaplain joined them. "He asked if our hearts were right with God," said Foster. "He wore an armband but carried no weapon. I appreciated that he risked his life to help us."

Foster was also impressed by Hollywood actors Mickey Rooney, Bob Hope and Ingrid Bergman who traveled to areas of war to entertain Allied troops.

In May 1945 Germany surrendered. When the Japanese emperor surrendered in August 1945, the war was officially over. Thousands of American soldiers were excited at the thought of returning home. Soldiers like Foster who did not yet have enough points to return, based on time in service, stayed in Europe to maintain peace. Finally, in April 1946 Foster had earned enough points to receive his discharge. He was issued a Purple Heart for sustaining injury during battle.

After the war, Foster worked for the U.S. Postal Service and a local fire department in Fort Wayne. He and Phyllis were married for 71 years before her death in March 2013. They were parents to two children. "I was happy to serve my country during the war," he said.

After four years of fighting, Allied troops break through the German barricade called the Siegfried Line, ca. 1945.

Ed Goetz—Army Air Corps/ Pacific

At 0300 hours in March 1945 Ed Goetz's B-29 flight crew of 12 was flying a 1,500-mile bombing mission from Saipan toward Japan. It was the 22nd bombing mission for this crew. Goetz, a native of Cincinnati, Ohio, served as flight engineer. He was responsible for maintaining mechanics for the big plane. The crew usually consisted of 11 members. The extra member that night was an observer for the bombardier.

Suddenly, the plane's propeller lost control. When the pilot nosed the plane up to slow it, the propeller ran faster. The pilot frantically asked the navigator for directions to Saipan. Upon being told the plane was close to the island of Agrihan, north of Saipan, the pilot headed in that direction. The radio operator sent the plane's location to the Saipan control tower shortly before flames shot out from the engine.

The pilot quickly instructed the crew, including Goetz, to don their parachutes and exit the plane. They quickly obeyed. The last crew member pilot had just jumped when the plane exploded. The dozen airmen dropped into darkness over the ocean, not knowing if they would ever see each other again.

> *Goetz didn't see or hear anyone from his crew. He worried that no one had survived the explosion.*

Goetz, 24, had flown bombing missions from Saipan to Japan since November 1944. Hoping to survive to someday be reunited with his wife whom he had married in October 1943 was uppermost in Goetz's mind as he zoomed toward earth in the darkness. Upon hitting the water, he tried to inflate the one-man life raft which was attached to the parachute harness but lost it. He cut the shroud lines of the harness before they could drag him under the surface.

Goetz scanned the sky and ocean for rescue. He prayed the plane's radio signals had been received. He didn't see or hear anyone from his crew and worried that no one had survived the explosion.

Shortly after sunrise, Goetz spotted a nearby island. He tried to swim towards it, but the early morning current caught his body and threw him against the boulders, gashing his head. When the waves threatened to suck him under again, Goetz, exhausted, gave up. He swam away from the rocks, trying to stay afloat, while awaiting rescue.

Surviving members of Goetz's (second from left) crew. Courtesy photo.

A few hours later, he was overjoyed when a sea plane flew over his location. Using the military mirror in his flight suit's knee pocket, Goetz focused on the sun to signal his location. He was thrilled when the pilot returned a flash signal indicating he had seen Goetz's signal.

Goetz next pulled a packet of light blue sea dye from another pocket of his flight suit, spreading it around to mark his location. Then he grasped an inflatable raft the rescue plane's crew dropped, hoping it would stay inflated for several hours. "I prayed my rescue would be soon," he said.

Unbeknownst to him, the plane had already picked up several members of his crew. After the rescue plane flew off with members of Goetz's crew, an American military ship, the USS Cook Inlet, spotted Goetz. "It was doing Dumbo duty, meaning it was looking for survivors," he said. The ship's crew helped him and other crew members safely aboard.

Hours later, after receiving medical attention and warm clothing and food, Goetz discovered the fate of his crew. Everyone survived the explosion but the plane's co-pilot, Col. Douglas Northrop. His body was never found, despite a week-long search by teams in the ocean and on Agrihan.

At the end of the extensive investigation as to the cause of the crash, it was decided a welding error inside the propeller's hub had caused oil that controlled the prop to pump out.

Goetz continued to fly missions through July 31, 1945, for a total of 37. He was discharged in November 1945 and resumed an education at the University of Cincinnati College of Engineering. In 1964 he moved to Indiana to work for Franklin Electric in Bluffton. He lives in Ossian. "I was glad to serve my country," he said.

A B-25 takes off from the deck of an aircraft carrier on its way to take part in the first U.S. air raid on Japan, April 1942.

Bonnie (Calhoun) Neuenschwander Habegger – Army Nurse

"We were told the Army needed nurses to relieve other nurses," said Bonnie Habegger of Berne. In May 1945 she was newly graduated as a registered nurse from Dallas Methodist Hospital. She had been born in Kaufman, Texas. After graduating from Kaufman High School in 1941, she planned on nursing as a career. The oldest of 10 children, she allowed the Army to cover the costs of her books, tuition, lodging. In return she would enlist in the Army to help with medical needs after the end of the war

Like her male soldier counterparts, Calhoun had to complete basic training. "We marched to meals, participated in daily exercises and learned to salute and stand at attention," she said. She was given the rank of 2nd lieutenant while caring for amputees at a military hospital in San Antonio and McCloskey General Hospital in Temple, Texas.

When the Army asked for volunteers to go overseas, Calhoun signed up. "I wanted to do what I could to help our country," she said. She was sent to Bremerhaven, Germany, on the SS John Ericsson. Calhoun didn't suffer from seasickness during the voyage and passed the time playing cards with other military personnel.

From Bremerhaven she traveled to Marmaton, France, where she worked at a station hospital caring for patients in scabies and venereal disease wards. Calhoun quickly established codes of behavior with patients. "I didn't like dirty jokes," she said. "If they said something nasty, I walked away." On Sundays Calhoun attended base chapel religious services. Howard Neuenschwander from Berne, Indiana, led the singing. He was an enlisted soldier who volunteered as the chaplain's assistant. One night, he asked Calhoun if he could walk her back to her room.

> ## "I didn't like dirty jokes. If the soldiers said something nasty, I walked away."

Calhoun had been warned about male soldiers. "We were told to be cautious because they had not seen women in a long time," she said. Howard Neuenschwander seemed different. He was in charge of the PX (post-exchange which served as a store on a military base). Calhoun noticed that he was popular. "Many people told me they thought he was a fine young man," she said. As a further caution, it was against Army protocol for officers to fraternize (date) enlisted personnel. "My girlfriend, who was also a nurse, dated an enlisted soldier and the Army separated them," she added. Still, Calhoun was willing to take a chance and she and Neuenschwander dated discreetly.

Then Calhoun received orders for a transfer to the 120th Station Hospital in Bayreuth, Germany. At the same time Neuenschwander received his discharge orders. The couple vowed to write letters. "I was sad to leave him," said Calhoun. Neuenschwander returned to Berne where he worked in an insurance business.

Calhoun kept busy working as head nurse on a prison ward at the hospital, caring for 30 American prisoners. She supervised five ward men while she performed administrative work. Calhoun could not talk to prisoners about why they were there, but she did establish ground rules. "They knew I did not appreciate crude talk or behavior," she said. While the prisoners conveyed attitudes of respect toward Calhoun, she always entered a cell to administer medicine with guard in tow.

The hospital was located in the part of Bavaria world-famous for the annual Bayreuth Festival with performances of operas by 19th-century German composer Richard Wagner. The heritage carried over at the hospital. "A cellist, violinist and pianist played classical music daily during our meals," she said. "I still love that type of music today."

Calhoun worked at the German hospital for approximately nine months. She was honorably discharged on June 15, 1948, at the rank of First Lieutenant.

On her way back to Texas from Boston, Calhoun visited Neuenschwander in Berne. They had been separated for 13 months, writing letters the entire time. Though she had dated other people, Calhoun had never found anyone she cared for like Neuenschwander. They were married in October 1948 at her Texan home.

She worked in private duty nursing for several years while they raised their four children in Berne. Howard founded an insurance business with his brother which he worked at until retirement. He died January 17, 1986. In December 2000 Bonnie married Grant Habegger, another World War II veteran. She has participated in Honor Flight for Northeast Indiana.

"I had a good experience as a soldier," she said. "I enjoyed my work and had fun. I was happy to serve my country. I did my duty and felt needed."

A wounded soldier is given blood plasma by a field medic after being wounded by shrapnel in Sicily, August 1943.

Simeon Hain – Navy / Pacific

"Fear has an odor," said Simeon Hain of Decatur. "It permeates your clothes and stinks. After getting back from a mission, I couldn't wait to take a shower."

Hain flew as a naval aviator during World War II. For eight months between 1944 and 1945 Hain flew 40 missions in a B-24, dropping bombs on selected locations in the Pacific. "On the day of a mission someone would wake me for patrol at 2 a.m. with a flashlight in my eyes," he said. "He pushed a clipboard under my nose telling me to sign that I had received my orders. Then I'd be given a briefcase filled with codes for the day, maps, charts, and other items pertinent for navigation."

After graduating from St. Joseph High School in Decatur in 1940, Hain worked two years in a supermarket before enlisting in the U.S. Navy. "The Navy was looking for aviators," he said. "I didn't have a college degree, which was required at the time, nor ridden in a plane or driven a car, but thought I'd give it a try." Hain made it through basic training and was admitted to the Civilian Pilots

Training program. At Ball State University Teacher's College he attended school in the morning, then had flight time in the afternoon.

Training in a Piper two-seater Cub was a challenge for Hain who battled motion sickness. "I didn't want to wash out of the program so I bought Mother Sill's Seasick Pills," he said. He studied math and physics to pass the academic sections of the training, then spent three months in a PBY airplane (patrol bomber aircraft) before entering flight training in Corpus Christi, Texas. He received his wings on September 25, 1943.

> *"Our crew could tell the location of the enemy because during flight we could hear Japanese music in their radios. When the music went off, they had us on their radar."*

Believing the Germans were planning to attack the United States mainland, the Navy assigned Hain the task of patrolling the St. John's area near Jacksonville, Fla., for submarines. Later, he was transferred to Norfolk, Va., for B-24 training. The B-24 was equipped not only with bombs but also with machine guns. By early 1944, Hain was flying combat missions in the Pacific Theater. "If we encountered enemy fire, I'd fly the plane at 200 knots (230 miles per hour), and the gunner would man the machine gun so it blazed," he said.

Hain's crew could usually tell the location of the enemy because during flight they could hear Japanese music in their radios. "When the music went off, we knew they had us on their radar," he said. One consolation of being pursued was the multitude of Chinese fishing junks in the ocean. "We knew if we crashed into the ocean, they would help us," he said.

Later that summer, he flew over Port Lyautey in Morocco and the Bay of Biscay in Spain. "Our mission was to watch on radar for enemy subs and eliminate them if possible," he said. He also flew for the Battle of the Philippines in October 1944 and across Saipan and Tinian.

In December 1944 Hain flew over the Bonin Islands, 500 miles southeast of Japan. He also bombed Iwo Jima during the terrible battle there in February 1945.

Another time Hain's crew became lost while flying over the ocean during a storm. When the plane's gas gauges showed the plane was low on fuel (it burned 200 gallons per hour), Hain looked for a place to land. Thinking he spotted mountains in the distance and that it might be the Marianas Chain, he pointed his plane in that direction.

When the clouds broke, Hain used the plane's flying instruments to identify their position which was near the island of Tinian. Requesting permission from the airfield on Tinian to land, Hain was relieved when the okay was given and he landed safely. The plane lost two engines during descent. "I was scared," he said, "especially when the dipstick in the gas gauge showed only 40 gallons left."

When Hain was discharged on November 1, 1945, he held the rank of Lt. Jr. Grade. He was presented with several medals and two Distinguished Flying Crosses. In July 1945, Hain married Patricia McConnell. The Hains became parents to two children.

After the war, Simeon Hain sold insurance. Despite the dangers presented to him while serving in the military, Hain always was thrilled with his job as a naval aviator. "For a young man there was nothing more exciting than flying," he said.

American pilots practiced flying formation in preparation for service in the war, September 1942.

Francis Holmes — Navy / Pacific

As a gunner at the Battle of Okinawa in spring 1945, Francis 'Link' Holmes shot 20-millimeter, 40-millimeter and six-inch artillery shells. "I lost the hearing in my right ear because of firing them," he said. Thousands of civilians were killed, wounded or committed suicide during that bloody conflict in the Pacific. "The Japanese believed in teaching soldiers to give up their lives for their country," he said. The result was the highest number of casualties in the Pacific Theater during the war. The Allies suffered more than 65,000, while the Japanese lost more than 100,000 soldiers.

Francis Holmes was 17 years old and not yet a graduate of Bluffton High School when he enlisted in the United States Navy in 1942. He had to talk his mother into helping him to enlist. "Since I was not 18 years old, she had to give her written permission," he said. His brother 'Peat' Holmes was fighting for the Army during the war. "We found out after the war that we were sometimes near each other but we never knew it," said Francis.

After completing basic training at Great Lakes Naval Training Center in Chicago, Holmes received training at Puget Sound Naval Yard in Bremerton, Washington.

He was assigned the rank of active seaman to the aircraft carrier USS Liscome Bay. Later, he transferred to the USS Casablanca, a Navy escort aircraft carrier. He sailed on this ship for 14 months before transferring to a destroyer squadron. Holmes was given orders to report to Brooklyn Naval Yard and later, Guantanamo Bay in Cuba. During the next three years, he was sent across the Pacific several times, encountering kamikaze fighters but amazingly surviving the war without injury.

Gunfire was not the only challenge for sailors. During Holmes' time in the Navy, he experienced several typhoons, one of which had waves that could have been 75 feet in height. Was he scared of drowning during the storms? "We were too busy trying to stay alive to be scared," he said.

Making friends with other sailors was not a common military practice, according to Holmes. "We didn't associate much with each other because being at war had taught us we might not be around for long," he said. That changed one day when Holmes spotted a sailor wearing a jacket with a familiar name on the back. It was Bill Bate, a former classmate at Bluffton High School. "He was the first person I had seen from home in three years," said Holmes. "We sat and talked about Bluffton all night."

> *"When we freed thousands of former POWs, we knew there would be many happy reunions with families who thought their loved ones were dead."*

The atomic bombings on cities of Hiroshima and Nagasaki finally convinced the Emperor of Japan to surrender in August 1945. As part of the Pacific Fleet, Holmes' crew participated in the invasion of South Korea and the liberation of a Japanese prisoner of war camp. "When we lowered the Japanese flag and freed thousands of people, it was an amazing thing to witness," said Holmes. "We knew there would be many happy reunions as former POWs returned to their families who thought their loved ones were dead."

While traveling the world as a sailor, Holmes achieved a rare distinction. Each American sailor who crossed the equator for the first time earned the unofficial nickname of Shellback. Sailors who crossed the International Date Line were given the nickname of Golden Dragon. A sailor who crossed the equator at the 180th meridian or International Date Line became a Golden Shellback. Holmes owns a cap with the Golden Shellback Cross stamped on the front.

By the time he was discharged on November 23, 1945, Holmes had served 34 months—30 of them overseas with no furlough. He sailed home on a transportation ship, USS Claiborne. Sailing was in his blood so Holmes re-enlisted in the Navy in December 1945. He was stationed as a gunner on a carrier at Tacoma, Washington until 1952 when he was honorably discharged for the second time.

In 1948 Holmes married Wilda Brickley of Bluffton. They became parents to seven children. Three of their sons joined the American military. As a civilian, Holmes worked in the maintenance department at Caylor-Nickel Hospital in Bluffton, while taking engineering classes at Indiana University in Fort Wayne. Later, he worked at Sterling Casting as an engineer, a career that lasted 35 years. Memories of his experiences in World War II remain at the back of Holmes' mind. "I wouldn't take nothing for the memories," he said, "but I wouldn't want to go through it again."

Holmes participated in Honor Flight for Northeast Indiana.

American gun crews scan the sky for enemy planes with their 5" guns aboard a Navy cruiser near the island of Mindoro in the Philippines, December 1944.

Loris "Bud' Jacobs – Army / Pacific

From 1943 until 1945 Wells County native Loris 'Bud' Jacobs was assigned to a field hospital in Iran. "The Allies provided supplies to the Russians along a 300-mile border during the Battle of Stalingrad," he said. "We were the back door for the people in Russia who the Germans were starving."

Jacobs, a graduate of East Union High School in Wells County, was drafted into the U.S. Army in August 1942. He completed basic training at Camp Barkley in Texas, then received training as a medic at Camp Butler near Durham, North Carolina. In January 1943 Jacobs and 7,500 other soldiers sailed from San Francisco on the RMS Mauritania. They landed at Pearl Harbor but left a few days later for New Zealand. "We zigzagged through the ocean to make it tougher for enemy subs to spot us," he said. A U.S. naval destroyer provided additional protection.

In March 1943 the ship picked up supplies and German prisoners of war in Australia before venturing to Iran. Sgt. Jacobs (he had been promoted) was assigned to help run the 25-bed 26th Field

Hospital located near the city of Ahwaz. German forces had made it difficult for Allied supplies to reach the impoverished people of Russia. The hospital -- a tent city -- was well-equipped with a pharmacy, lab, motor pool, and mess area. Jacobs was in charge of the duty roster at the hospital.

The tent hospital moved often according to need. It stayed one year at Hamadan, then Andamish and a year later, Khorramshahr, a port city located approximately 10 kilometers north of Abadan. Six months later, it was established at Karimabad, a village in northwest Iran. "At each site we had good relationships with the Iranian people," said Jacobs. "We called them Sunis and they called us Johnnys."

Living in the desert was not easy. "The Iranians had a saying about the desert heat," said Jacobs. "They said, 'In July flies die. In August Johnny die'." At that time the Shah of Iran was friendly to the U.S. and visited the troops. "He and his wife watched a USO show with us," said Jacobs. The Shah allowed tours for the troops through his palace in Tehran. Jacobs was impressed with the elegant home. "The Shah's throne was shaped like a peacock and embedded with jewels," he said.

> ### "At the bridge at Remagen our trucks had men standing in the turret with machine guns."

Desert animals wandered around the tent cities. At one location soldiers adopted three gazelles as pets. "We named one Bambi," said Jacobs. Another time he saw a caravan of nomads riding camels through the area.

In March 1945 Jacobs' unit sailed through the Suez Canal into the Mediterranean Sea. The soldiers crossed to Marseilles, France, to Camp Calais. In Germany Jacobs' platoon, attached to Patton's 7th Army, encountered opposition as it attempted to cross a bridge over the Rhine River at the village of Remagen. "Each truck had a man standing in the turret with a machine gun to protect us," he said.

After a difficult fight (Hollywood made the battle into a movie, The Bridge at Remagen), Allies gained control of the bridge and traveled through the cities of Stuttgart, Heidelberg, and Mannheim. The last town had been nearly leveled by bombs, and 120,000 people were killed. The 7th Army commandeered a school building to set up a station hospital. Jacobs worked at the hospital until Germany surrendered in May 1945. When the Japanese emperor surrendered in August, the war was officially over.

Lacking the required number of points to go home, Jacobs enrolled in college courses arranged by the American military. "The Army arranged for 4,000 of us to stay in hotels and beaches on the Riviera," he said. "I studied public speaking and journalism."

Jacobs' courses were interrupted six weeks later as he had earned the required number of points to be discharged. He left France in November 1945, arrived in New York, and traveled by train to Camp Atterbury in southern Indiana. He was discharged on December 3, 1945. Jacobs received two battle stars for his service in Central Europe and southern France and a medal from the Russian government for his help in assisting their country.

Jacobs married in 1948. He and his wife Polly Stokes lived in Fort Wayne and became parents to two children. He worked at International Harvester in Fort Wayne before retiring. Jacobs participated with Flight of Northeast Indiana. "I was glad to serve my country," he said.

Nurses from a field hospital arrive in France after three years of service overseas, August 1944.

Vernon Kaehr — Army / Europe

"Part of my responsibilities with the 44th Infantry Division, 3rd Battalion, 114th Infantry was to pick up the dead," said Vernon Kaehr of Bluffton. He was stationed one-half mile from the front line of battle along the Maginot Line in France in 1944. The Maginot Line was a series of concrete fortifications and obstacles France had constructed along its borders. Unfortunately, the country had still been overtaken by Germany. Fierce battles ensued as the United States and other Allied countries tried to liberate the French people.

Kaehr was born in 1923 in Ferndale, Michigan. His family moved to Bluffton when he was a young boy and he graduated from Lancaster High School in 1942. He was drafted into military service with the U.S. Army in February 1943.

After passing a physical examination at Fort Benjamin Harrison in Indianapolis, Kaehr was assigned to the Infantry, 37-mm Antitank Regiment and sent to Fort Lewis in Washington for basic training. "We were trained to shoot M1 carbine rifles," he said. Upon being granted leave in September 1943, Kaehr returned to Bluffton to marry his high school sweetheart, Mary Ann Steffen.

The couple drove to Fort Lewis where Kaehr was transferred to the supply department. "I helped the supply sergeant locate items our soldiers needed like weapons, parts, boots," he said. At times he also worked as a Weapons Repairman.

Mary Ann found a job at the shipyards riding a bike to deliver messages between offices. A few months later, Vernon was sent to Louisiana for special training and Mary Ann returned to Bluffton. At Camp Champney his pack weighed 30 pounds, including his rifle. "At night we ran 20 miles with our packs," he said.

In October 1944 Kaehr's troop ship left Boston Harbor, bound for Cherbourg, France. During the 10-day crossing, many soldiers were seasick. Kaehr escaped the malady, but was aware the ship was a target for German subs. "Our ship dropped depth bombs looking for the enemy," he said. "We traveled as part of a convoy with other ships for protection."

> *"When our plane was shot down over Germany, another soldier and I survived but had to scrounge for food."*

In France the troops moved to the Maginot Line, then Frankenstein, Germany. It was winter and the Army stayed alert for Screaming Meemies -- nickname for German rocket artillery. Once, a shell landed 15 feet from Kaehr but didn't explode. Another close call occurred when a Jeep he was riding in flipped after being shelled. Kaehr was struck on the chin by a piece of ice but was otherwise unhurt.

Kaehr witnessed an American army sergeant die while trying to demonstrate how to defuse a German mine. Two other soldiers standing nearby were also killed. "They were good men," he said. Still another crisis occurred when a plane Kaehr was riding in was shot down over Germany. He and another soldier survived but were stranded in an abandoned village. With no provisions and little knowledge of the area, the two scrounged for food. Kaehr knew how to dress a chicken so after catching a loose hen, he prepared it and the two ate, along with apples from a nearby tree. Eventually they made their way back to Allied lines.

For a year, Sgt. Kaehr traveled with his regiment through France, Germany and Austria. By the time the Allies crossed the Danube River in spring 1945, Germany was on the retreat. Mary Ann wrote letters daily. Kaehr replied, though parts of his missives were censored (blacked out) to keep the enemy from knowing the Allies' plans, should the letter fall into the wrong hands.

Kaehr was in a village in southern Austria in May 1945 when Germany surrendered. He was shipped back to the U.S. and stationed at Fort Smith in Arkansas on August 9, 1945, when the Japanese emperor surrendered. "It was a relief to know we would not have to fight in Japan," he said.

Kaehr was discharged in November 1945. Among his souvenirs were a German helmet and pistol, Nazi flag, German medal and his uniform. Kaehr owned a dairy supply business in Bluffton before retiring in 1987. Vernon and Mary Ann celebrated 70 years of marriage in September 2013. They are parents to four daughters. Kaehr participated with Honor Flight for Northeast Indiana "If needed, I would go in the service again," he said.

American troops advance into a Belgian town under the protection of a heavy tank, September 1944.

Arnold Keuneke – Army, Africa / Europe

While enrolled at Wren High School in Wren, Ohio, Arnold Keuneke signed up for a correspondence course in electricity. Born in Adams County in 1920, he had moved with his family to Ohio as a child. After two years, Keuneke dropped out of high school. "There was nothing left to learn," he said. He continued studying electricity while working at Wayne Knitting Mill in Fort Wayne.

In 1941 Arnold married Louise Ensley. The couple lived in an apartment in Fort Wayne until February 1942 when Keuneke was drafted into the U.S. Army. After completing basic training at Camp Crowder in Joplin, Missouri, Keuneke was sent to Midland Radio School in Kansas City, Mo.; radar school at Camp Murphy in West Palm Beach, Florida; and Drew Field in Tampa.

In January 1943, he and other American troops left on a boat from Port Andrew in New York City for Africa. In Oran, Tech Sgt. Keuneke was attached to the 12th Air Force in the Signal Corps. "We were in charge of maintaining a 588 radar unit," he said. Radar systems used 300-foot steel masts to emit radio signals. "The radar helped Allied pilots receive signals to alert them about enemy aircraft in the area."

Located on a hill over the Mediterranean Sea in the South Tibesa desert, the unit operated solely under Keuneke's expertise. Part of his tasks required climbing the unit for repairs and working around wiring for bombs. "I had no fear of heights," he said. "We were careful." He was also available to work with any military branch that needed him on temporary duty. The following year an assistant trained in radar was assigned to help him manage the large radar station and a smaller one. Keuneke also installed a radar set in B-25 planes.

> **"We were in charge of maintaining a 588 radar unit. Radar helped Allied pilots receive signals to alert them about enemy aircraft."**

Keuneke was often in the line of fire on the front line but escaped injury. "Those bullets didn't have my name on them," he said. Another time he was not so lucky at escaping injury. While repairing a tire, the seal blew and clipped him in the eye. Keuneke did not seek medical aid at the mobile hospital unit. Instead, he asked the company cook to stitch up the injury. Afterward, he drove a 2.5-ton truck with vision limited to one eye to the port city of Algiers.

Malaria was a constant threat for the troops in Africa. When Keuneke and his assistant were advised to swallow pills to prevent the dreaded illness, they did so but within hours, Keuneke felt sick. He quit taking the medicine and felt better, never contracting the dreaded disease. Unfortunately, his assistant developed malaria. As there was no hospital around Constantine where they were stationed, the assistant had to endure the illness on his own. Though he survived, he died of malarial symptoms five years after the war.

From Africa, Keuneke was sent to Pisa and Corsica in Italy. While there, he befriended an Italian family. When he offered candy to their two little boys, the parents begged Keuneke to adopt the boys. "They were so poor and hungry and they thought I could provide a better home for their sons in America," he said. Keuneke refused the offer but was moved by their plight.

In August 1945 the Japanese emperor surrendered and the war was over. Keuneke had served his country for three years and soon received papers to be shipped home. He returned to Norfolk, Va., on a liberty ship in September 1945. He recalled Salvation Army volunteers on hand when his ship came in to harbor. "They offered us candy and cigarettes," he said.

After the war, Keuneke worked at Dana Corporation in Fort Wayne as an electrician. He also operated a farm outside of Columbia City. Keuneke and his wife became parents to five children.

Arnold Keuneke brought home two unusual souvenirs. Using a pocket knife and hack saw, he constructed a photo album from parts of a German bomber that was shot down. The album is full of photos taken by Keuneke during his time in service. Keuneke also used a metal cup issued to him at Fort Benjamin Harrison to etch names of places he was stationed throughout his military service.

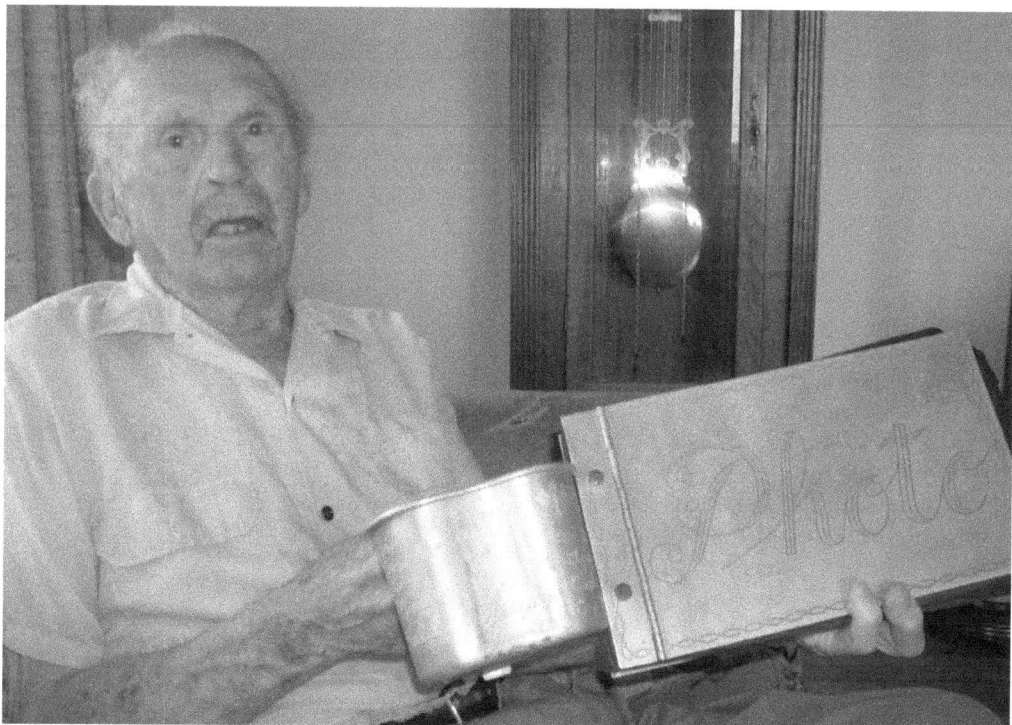

American troops leap from a landing craft to storm a North African beach during amphibious maneuvers, ca. 1944.

Ruth (Cooper) Licking – Army WAC

The bombing of Pearl Harbor on December 7, 1941, changed American life dramatically. The United States government instituted the military draft, requiring men to leave their homes and jobs to fight in locales around the world. The need for men to serve overseas created vacancies in many offices and factories. Desperate to fill those vacant jobs, the American government urged women to go to work.

Ruth Cooper of Marion, N.C. was intrigued at the thought of enlisting in the newly-created Women's Army Auxiliary Corps (WAAC). "It didn't terrify me as much as it thrilled me," she said. "I believed the good Lord intended me to be a soldier." By the following year, she had applied for a position. To be accepted in the WAAC, a woman had to be between the ages of 21 and 45 and at least 60 inches tall. Cooper was 22 years old and 63 inches tall. So far, so good.

The problem came with the weight requirement. A WAAC had to weigh at least 105 pounds. Cooper weighed 98 pounds. Upon learning of her determination to serve in the army, the physician administering physical examinations allowed Cooper to wear her shoes, purse and coat on the scale to pass the exam.

In March 1943 Cooper traveled by bus to Fort Oglethorpe, Ga., for basic training. She and the other females rose daily at 0600 hours to fall out for roll call. They marched to the field for drill and physical training and attended courses on map reading, defense against chemical warfare and air attacks, military customs and courtesy. Part of the WAACs' training was in neatness and orderliness.

> *"In the Army we were told there were two ways to live. I was happy as a soldier living the Army way."*

Each WAAC was issued an Army blanket, sheets, pillow, wall locker and a footlocker placed at the base of the bed. "We were taught that everything had a place," Cooper said. The women slept in barracks lined with rows of bunks. Each bed was made so a quarter would bounce on it. "If your bed was not properly made, you were gigged, or punished, and made to do it over. I was careful never to have that happen to me."

After basic training, Cooper volunteered to serve overseas, but was assigned to a clerical position at Kelly Field in San Antonio. "I kept track of paperwork for officers' transfers and those headed overseas," she said. Her assignment at HQ earned her the rank of corporal and later, sergeant. Her pay was $78 a month. On August 31, 1943, the WAAC service disbanded and all of the WAAC's were dismissed. Those who wanted to re-enlist could do so the following day in the Women's Army Corps (WAC). Cooper was one of more than 45,000 WAACs who re-enlisted.

In December 1943, Cooper received a special honor when the other WACs at Kelly Field chose her as their representative for 'Miss Victory'. "I was thought to be the female counterpart to the male soldier," she said. "The other WACs saw me as someone who was willing to work hard, sacrificially and with little fuss." Cooper and two other WACs from neighboring bases were recognized at a military ball during which the acclaimed Andrews Sisters sang.

In June 1944, Cooper was with a group of girlfriends when she met some soldiers, including Tech Sgt. Bill Licking. He had been stationed in Panama for three years and was now stationed at Kelly Field in an administrative position. Licking was from Greensburg, Ind. During the next several months, Cooper and Licking saw each other often. They fell in love and decided to marry in the base chapel on February 17, 1945. Because of gas shortages and difficulty in travel, neither had family present. Cooper borrowed a wedding dress from a fellow WAC. Licking's solid gold wedding band cost $45. It was engraved with their names and wedding date.

The war ended in August 1945. Ruth was discharged in September and Bill was discharged a month later. They moved to Greensburg, then Bluffton, where they operated a men's clothing store for 27 years. They became parents to four children. In 2010 Licking participated in Honor Flight for Northeast Indiana.

"In the Army we were told there were two ways to live," she said. "I was happy as a soldier living the Army way. If anybody would ask me to do it again, I would. I might not have done as much for my country as an American soldier stationed overseas, but I filled a gap. As little as it might have been, I helped. That's what it was all about."

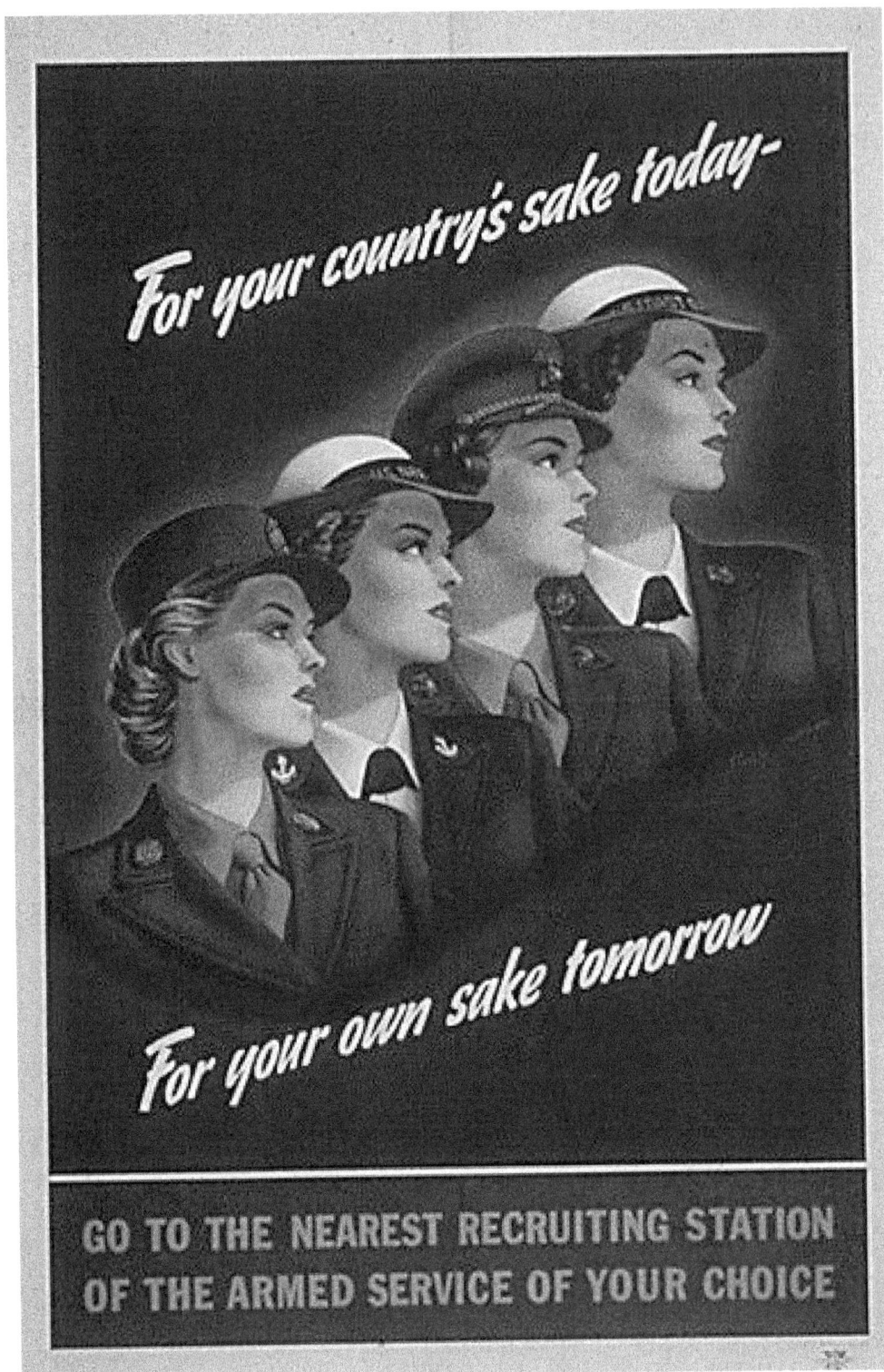

Posters encourage young women to enlist in various military branches to help fill administrative, nursing and other jobs.

Carl Lee Mankey — Marines / Pacific

In June 22, 1944, Marine Pfc. Carl Mankey led 20 men from his squadron up a mountain in Saipan in the Mariana Islands. Mankey's goal was to destroy a Japanese machine gun nest that had fired for hours on Allied troops. Disregarding heavy fire from the enemy, Mankey moved into the open to shoot with his rifle and throw grenades, hoping to disrupt the firing. Failing to hit the target, Mankey refused to give up. He returned to the machine gun nest, repeating his brave actions. This time he completely destroyed it.

Mankey, a graduate of Kirkland High School in Adams County, was employed as a truck driver and living near Craigville when he enlisted in the Marine Corps in January 1943. Why did he choose the Marines? "I figured they were the toughest soldiers," he said. Mankey trained in San Diego at the Marine Corps Recruit Depot where he was assigned to the 2nd Marine Division, 6th Regiment, Company B. He received more training in New Zealand before experiencing his first look at war.

In February 1943 Mankey's squadron was sent to Guadalcanal in the southern Solomon Islands as replacements for Allied troops fighting there. However, his group had lost so many men from sickness that they were ordered to remain aboard ship. From where he stood watching the battle from on deck, Mankey was horrified at the sight of Allied soldiers falling from mortar attack and bullets. "It was worse watching it from the ship than being on land," he said.

Disregarding heavy fire from the enemy, Mankey threw grenades at the machine gun nest, completely destroying it.

On the island of Tarawa in November 1943 the fighting was again intense. The U.S. needed to take the Marianas Islands to set up air bases to support operations across the mid-Pacific.

Though the battle only lasted three days with an Allied triumph, approximately 6,000 soldiers died on both sides. "We heard the number of soldiers who died on Tarawa was worse per mile than anywhere else in the Pacific," said Mankey. He was one of those wounded on the island when a bomb exploded and he suffered a concussion. He was sent to a Hawaiian hospital for four months to recuperate.

In June 1944 Mankey was again in the midst of war, this time on the island of Saipan. He was injured a second time when an enemy bullet pierced his water flask, ricocheting off of his rifle and removing the end of his nose. He recuperated at a hospital in Saipan before returning to fight on Tinian in August.

Allied forces were successful at vanquishing Japanese forces in all of these conflicts. Mankey saw more action on the island of Iwo Jima in late winter 1945 and Okinawa in April.

Note: The Battle of Iwo Jima is perhaps best known for Joe Rosenthal's photograph of the raising of the U.S. flag on top of the 545-foot Mount Suribachi by six soldiers. The photograph records the second flag-raising on the mountain, both of which took place on the fifth day of the 35-day battle. Rosenthal's photograph promptly became a symbol of the war and is one of the most common photos produced of the war.

After three years of island hopping and surviving several brutal battles, Corp. Mankey was ready to go home. He was discharged December 14, 1945. During the war, Mankey was paid $66 per month for his military service. At the time of discharge he was given five cents per mile for travel allowance from Naval Station

Great Lakes in Illinois, in addition to $260 issued to soldiers as standard pay for his rank.

In 1947 Carl married Dolores Lengerich. They became parents to six children. After the war, Carl returned to his job as a truck driver in Fort Wayne. Mankey participated in Honor Flight for Northeast Indiana in 2011.

Mankey's thoughts about his nearly three years of overseas military service are succinct. "It was a heck of an experience," he said. "We need to support today's American military and its work."

Marine machine gunners push back Japanese soldiers on the island of Cape Gloucester, New Guinea, January 1944.

Robert Dale Morrissey — Army / Pacific

Robert Dale Morrissey's life was saved during World War II -- not by a fellow soldier but by a four-legged friend.

Morrissey, a 1940 Bluffton High School graduate, was drafted into the U.S. Army in October 1942. Previously, he had trained at an Army National Guard unit in New Castle, Ind., while working in a shoe store.

Morrissey, who was promoted to sergeant, practiced Louisiana Maneuvers, then mountain training in Arizona and California. In 1943 Morrissey, assigned to the 32nd (Red Arrow) Division, boarded a ship with thousands of other American soldiers at San Francisco. Sailing under the Golden Gate Bridge into the Pacific Ocean, they headed to New Guinea.

By the time the ship arrived two weeks later, the island had been cleared of Japanese fighters, though snipers were still in the area. "Some of them didn't believe the war was over," said Morrissey.

The appearance of cannibals on the island shocked Morrissey. "The native men of New Guinea appeared to be 12 feet tall and didn't wear clothes," he said. "They assisted the Allies by moving large pieces of metal to help build runways for the Army Air Corps."

In the Philippines Morrissey was promoted to staff sergeant of the 128th Infantry Personnel section. His duties as company clerk included reporting the names of soldiers killed in action. "I wrote letters of condolence to their families," he said. "It was rough, but I did the best I could."

The Red Arrow Division fought on the Villa Verde Trail in Luzon. Morrissey and the other soldiers divided the natives into two groups. "They either fought for the Japanese or were against them," said Morrissey. Filipinos against the Japanese helped the Allies by washing their clothes and preparing meals. "We never ate anything cooked by the Army while there," he added.

> *When the soldiers' pet dog Caribou smelled smoke, she quickly awoke the soldiers with frantic barking.*

One bright note with eternal consequences occurred when a Filipino wash lady gave a short-haired, black and white pup to Morrissey's outfit. The soldiers named the pup of unknown origin Caribou and fed it with an eye dropper until it was old enough to drink from a bowl. They smuggled Caribou aboard a landing ship leaving for Japan. "Many unauthorized things went on in the Army, but pets kept the soldiers happy," he said.

In Yamaguchi Morrissey's unit settled into an army camp with buildings of knotty pine ceilings and walls. One night, after the soldiers had gone to sleep, the wiring caused a fire and the wooden building quickly ignited.

Caribou smelled the smoke first and quickly awoke the soldiers with her frantic barking. Morrissey and all but two of the other enlisted soldiers safely evacuated the building. Sadly, two officers perished in the fire. According to a military news report, "the dog became a mascot of the 128th, rating a cherished spot in the barracks, chow line and greatest of all, the heart of the soldiers."

When the war ended in August 1945, the city of Hiroshima was still smoking from the dropping of the bomb as Morrissey's unit drove through days later. He had been re-assigned to perform clerical duties until his discharge. Though saddened by the effects of the bombing, Morrissey believes it was for the good. "If President Truman had not made that order, I don't think we would be here today," he said.

Morrissey resumed his clerical duties before being told he could go home. On Christmas Day 1945 he crossed the International Dateline headed for Seattle. The first thing he did upon reaching America was to get his shoes shined.

He was discharged from Camp Atterbury in southern Indiana on January 11, 1946.

After Morrissey returned to Bluffton, he resumed his job at the shoe store, eventually managing the shop with his future father-in-law as the Haiflich and Morrissey Shoe Store. He and his wife, Evelyn, became parents to four children.

Reflecting back on his time in military service, Morrissey said, "I felt as though I had been through the school of hard knocks for four years."

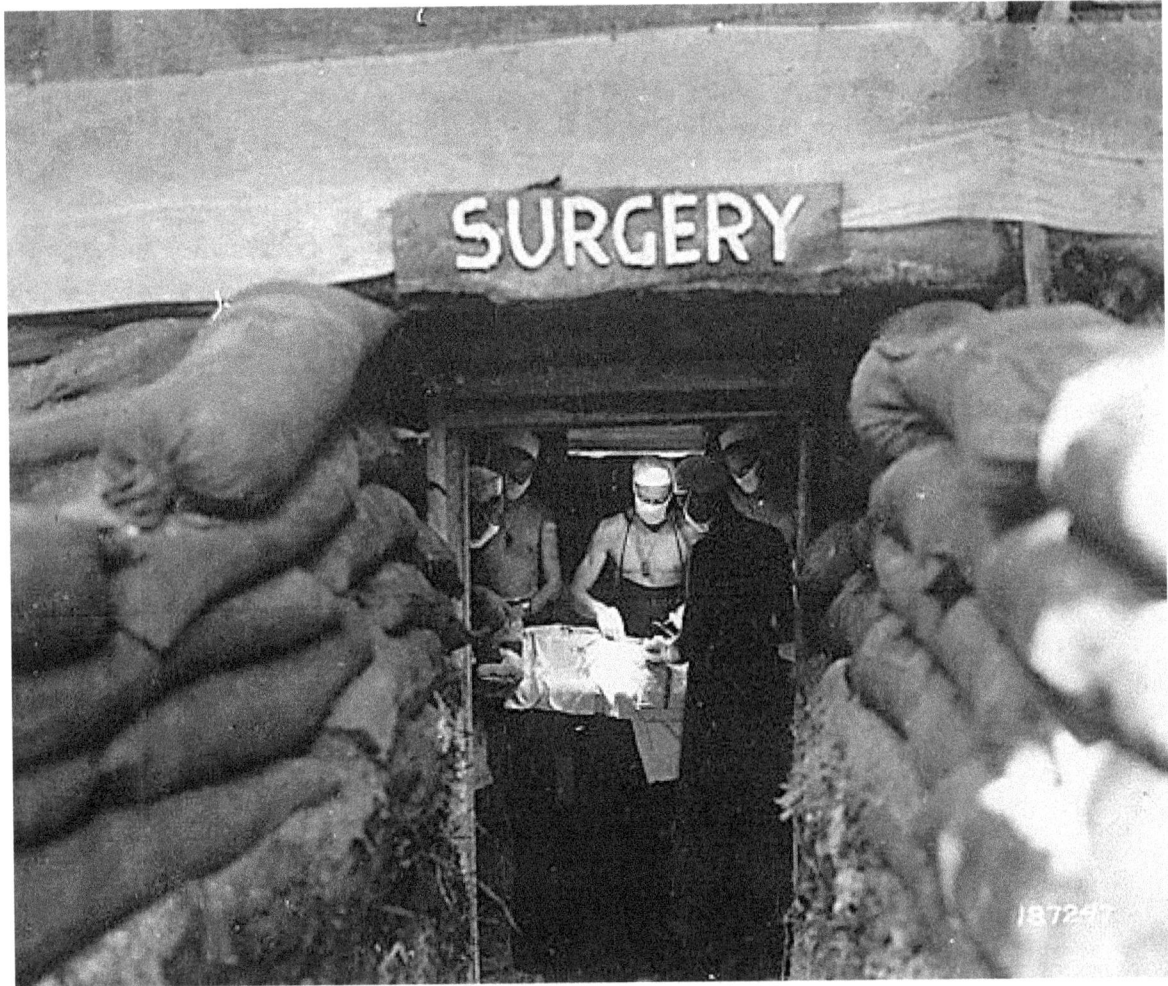

In an underground surgery area behind the front lines on Bougainville, an American Army doctor operates on a U.S. soldier wounded by a Japanese sniper, December 1943.

Ervin Moser – Army / Pacific

"Daily I witnessed injured soldiers airlifted in from the front lines," said Ervin Moser of Bluffton. "Shells flew overhead from both sides." Moser referred to his experiences as a medic working in a tent hospital in the Philippines during World War II. Sadly, he often treated people he knew. "Three of the guys in my company were killed," he added.

Moser graduated from Bluffton High School in 1941 and worked in his family's restaurant until being drafted into the U.S. Army in 1944. During basic training at Fort Bragg in South Carolina, Moser and other American soldiers were trained to shoot M1 carbine rifles. He earned a Sharpshooter badge. Having scored high on tests for medical aptitude, Moser was sent for medical training at Camp Grant in Ill. He completed additional training at Fort Lewis in Washington, Camp Ellis in Ill. and Camp Stoman in California.

When Moser finally shipped out via converted troop ship to New Guinea, then Leyte in the Philippines, he, like many soldiers, suffered from seasickness. "The waves were often 40 feet high," he said. Pfc. Moser stayed one year at Leyte, working at the 312th General Hospital, a tent hospital filled with 300 beds.

Though most of his time was spent working with medicine, Moser also assisted in the hospital's kitchen. "My sister, Goldie Moser, had run a restaurant in Bluffton so I knew how to cook," he said. Much of the military's food was imported. "We got fresh eggs and decent meat from Australia. We also peeled a lot of potatoes and ate beans."

A nickelodeon with a working record player in the officer's building provided musical entertainment to off-duty soldiers. "If you put in a nickel, you could hear the song, 'I Wonder Who's Kissing Her Now'," he said. "That song made us soldiers feel sad."

One day Corp. Moser (he had been promoted) was working in the kitchen when he began to feel feverish and weak. A doctor confirmed Moser had contracted the dreaded disease of yellow fever. With no appetite he lost 30 pounds, eventually weighing only 125 pounds. When Moser was finally dismissed from the hospital, it was August 1945 and the war was over. Hitler and the Japanese emperor had surrendered. Soldiers were allowed to return home, based on points earned for time in service.

Unable to return to the hospital because he had been ill, Moser was assigned the task of guarding Japanese prisoners of war in Manila. "We assigned them daily work details of cleaning up the yard and custodial tasks," he said. When it was finally his turn to go home, Moser traveled on a liberty ship from the Philippines to Olympia, Wash. He then flew to Indianapolis where he was officially discharged on May 7, 1946.

> *"A nickel in the record player provided musical entertainment to soldiers. The song, 'I Wonder Who's Kissing Her Now' made us feel sad."*

One souvenir Moser took home was a bit unusual – a monkey. "The nurses at the hospital gave it to me," he said. "I named it 'Rita' after Hollywood actress and pin-up girl Rita Hayworth." Other soldiers took home parrots. "We soldiers took turns staying on deck at night to watch the animals."

In 1946 Moser married Lula Fiechter, a young woman from his hometown whom he had known before the war. The two had written dozens of letters during the war and were married 51 years before Lula's death in 1998. The Mosers lived in Bluffton and owned a farm machinery dealership. They were parents to one daughter.

Decades after his involvement in the Pacific during World War II, Moser applied for his records from the National Personnel Records Center. Unfortunately, on July 12, 1973, a fire at the center destroyed approximately 18 million official military personnel files. Moser's was one record salvaged from the fire. He displays his medals and a copy of his record, burnt around the edges, in a case in his home.

In May 2014 Moser participated in Honor Flight for Northeast Indiana. "It was a big day, but they treated us well," he said.

Moser has positive remembrances of his time in the Army. "We made out the best we could," he said. "I made good friends there and we kept busy, but it was good. I don't regret being there."

U.S. troops go over the side of a combat transport vessel to enter landing barges to begin an invasion at Bougainville, November 1943.

Roger Myers – Army Air Corps

During World War II, Roger Myers of Fort Wayne worked on one top secret weapon and was nearly involved with another.

After graduating from Coldwater High School in Ohio, Myers enlisted in the Army Air Corps in December 1942. He was sent to Miami Beach but, due to the need for replacements of soldiers, basic training that was supposed to last six weeks was reduced to a few lectures.

At Scott Field near Belleville, Ill., Myers received training as a radio operator. Seven weeks later, he was back in Fla. at Tyndall Field in Panama City to attend aerial gunnery school.

"We started with BB guns because some guys had never shot a gun," he said. "We worked up to guns with 50-cal. bullets and a projectile the size of my thumb that could shoot two miles."

They also shot machine guns that fired six rounds a second.

79

When Myers was done at Tyndall, he enrolled in flight training. At Denver, Salt Lake City, Santa Ana, Calif., and Washington State College Myers was taught military conduct and courtesy, German and Japanese languages, and clothing etiquette. Two months later, he was assigned the crew position of bombardier. "The military made the choices for us between pilots, navigators or bombardiers," he said.

At Carlsbad, N.M., Myers graduated from bombardier school, earning his wings as a flight crew member. During his time there, he trained nine flight crew members from China. "I could not understand them, but they could understand me as I told them how to fly," he said. China had been in conflict with Japan since the 1930s. Myers' yearbook from Carlsbad contains photos of the Chinese pilots he trained. He then spent four months at ground school for the Norden bombsight. This was a top-secret weapon designed to ensure accuracy in dropping bombs.

> *"A major called me to his office. He asked me what I knew about bats."*

At Carlsbad Myers was nearly involved with another secret project, one that could have replaced the atomic bomb. It began with his upbringing in Coldwater. His dad had been a flour miller. One day the local Catholic priest knocked on the door of their home. The priest wanted help in dealing with bats in the church belfry since Roger's dad had often dealt with them at the mill.

Roger helped his father set up crocks of cyanide to kill the bats. Later, when he was in the military, he wrote to his father, asking about the bats as a topic of conversation. A few days later, Myers was surprised when he was called to a room to speak to a major. "He asked me what I knew about bats," he said. Myers realized military personnel had read his mail. "I told the major I knew how to kill bats and that was all," he added. He never heard more about it until years later at a bombardier reunion.

It seemed Carlsbad Caverns was known for its large bat population. Some military personnel had thought to use bats in a bombing exercise. "They planned to attach incendiary devices to the bats' throats and drop them over Japan," he said. "The bats would seek shadowy places and explode at night. They were thought to be more humane for civilians than an atomic bomb." When the U.S. decided to use the atomic bombs in an effort to end the war with Japan, the bat bombs idea was dropped.

In August 1945 2nd Lt. Myers was sent to Las Vegas Army Air field where he flew B-29s until his discharge in December 1945. Upon arriving home in Coldwater, he was delighted to discover not only had his three older brothers survived the war, he outranked them. "I was the only one with a commission," he said.

After the war, Myers worked for Chicago & Southern Airlines (today Delta Airlines) at Fort Wayne International Airport (then called Baer Field Airport) for 44 years. In 1949 Myers married Vonola Barkley and they became parents to three sons. In 1984 Myers helped establish the Greater Fort Wayne Aviation Museum, Inc., located at FWA. He co-authored a book about the history of aviation in Fort Wayne.

With a lifelong interest in aviation Myers remembers where it all began. "I'm proud of the fact that I served in the Army Air Corps during WWII," he said. "It was a necessary function and I did my best."

In 2012 Myers participated in Honor Flight for Northeast Indiana.

A Chinese soldier guards a line of American P-40 fighter planes, painted with the Shark face emblem of the 'Flying Tigers,' at a flying field in China, ca. 1942.

Margaret Ray Ringenberg -- Women Airforce Service Pilots (WASP)

"Don't quit now!" pleaded 21-year-old Margaret 'Maggie' Ray of Hoagland. Carefully she steered the Bamboo Bomber through the skies over Washington D.C., easing back on the throttle. Peering out the window at the left engine, she was alarmed when a sudden vibration shook the aircraft. Scanning the instrument panel, she was relieved to see both engines working, though the left seemed dangerously close to failure.

Below, she could see the Potomac River and in the distance the Capitol Building. It was 1944 and Ray was a member of the Women Airforce Service Pilots (WASP). After graduating from Hoagland High School in 1940, Ray had obtained her private pilot's license. In 1943 she applied and was accepted into the WASP program in Sweetwater, Texas. Women pilots handled a multitude of tasks stateside, including the transport of military personnel and supplies. They also tested new aircraft and delivered planes. These services allowed male pilots to fly combat missions overseas.

> **Ray radioed to the control tower that she planned to land. As the wheels touched down, gas poured over the left engine.**

As a WASP, Ray had passed check rides in a PT-19, BT-13, AT-6 and UC-78. She earned her instrument rating in a DC-3 and co-piloted a B-24 and C-54. "My favorite plane was anything with wings and a propeller," she said. "Every day was a new adventure." She thrilled in taking new, untested planes from the factories to military bases where they were needed. But flying old planes to the 'bone yard' could be nerve-wracking. She had picked up this twin-engine Cessna at Bradley Field in Conn. Her assignment was to deliver it to its final resting place in Montgomery, Ala.

After several minutes of studying the ever-increasing vibration, Ray radioed to the control tower. "I'm going to land," she said. She preferred that to bailing out. "Cleared to land," she heard as the wheels touched down. She felt relief until she looked out the window. Gas poured over the left engine. She quickly shut down the engines and exited without mishap.

From 1943-1944 Ray and other WASP flew 60 million miles of operational flights across the U.S. from aircraft factories to ports of embarkation and military training bases. They also towed targets for live anti-aircraft artillery practice, simulated strafing missions, and transported cargo.

Despite their skills, the WASP were considered civilians and thus entitled to no military benefits. By summer 1944 Allied pilots were sent home seeking pilot positions. With their return Congress disbanded the WASP program. Ray enlisted in the Reserves, earning the rank of 1st Lt. She was discharged in 1947.

After the war, Ray gave flying lessons at Smith Field in Fort Wayne where she had learned to fly. She also flew for hire for area businesses. In 1946 she married Capt. Morris Ringenberg of the Army Corps of Engineering. They lived in Leo and became parents to two children. In 2007 Margaret Ringenberg was picked during the Gathering of Eagles at Maxwell Air Force Base in Alabama as one of 16 pilots who attained recognition in the field of aviation.

The following year she was inducted into the International Women in Aviation Pioneer Hall of Fame at the Women in Aviation International Conference in San Diego.

In her 70s she completed two world air races. She was made a member of The Ninety Nines, Experimental Aircraft Association, Air Race Classic Association, Smith Field Association, and speaker for NASA Distinguished Lecture Series.

Television newscaster Tom Brokaw featured Ringenberg in a chapter of his New York Times book, The Greatest Generation. Her life is also chronicled in her autobiography Girls Can't Be Pilots (Daedalus Press 1998) and a book written by her daughter Marsha J. Wright: Maggie Ray: World War II Air Force Pilot (Pen & Publish 2007). (Excerpts from the latter book were used in the opening of this story with permission of the author.)

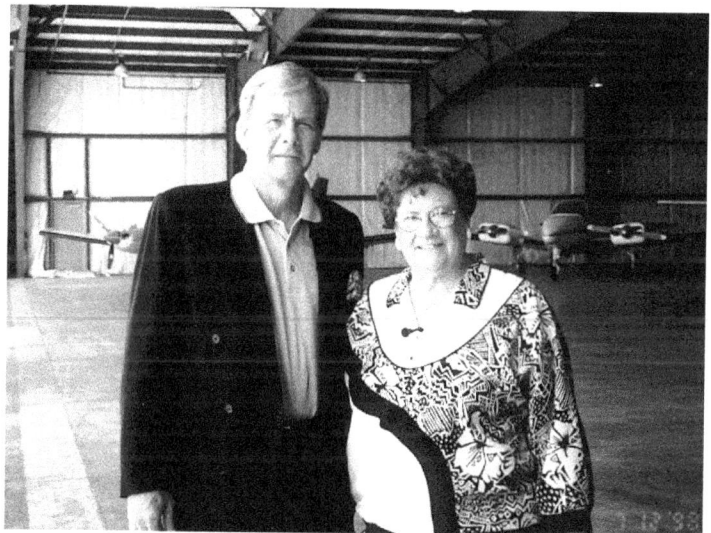

Ringenberg died of natural causes in 2008 in Oshkosh, Wis., at its world-famous air show. During her lifetime, she logged more than 40,000 flight hours in hundreds of aircraft. In her later years Ringenberg experienced hearing loss as a result of flying in older planes during the war. The disability did not dim her enthusiasm about her military career. "My dad, Albert Ray, always said there was nothing too hard for me to accomplish," she said. "He believed I could do anything I put my mind to, including becoming a pilot. I proved him right."

Ringenberg dropped leaflets like this one over the city of Fort Wayne following Japan's surrender in August 1945.

Leo Scheer – Navy / Europe and Pacific

As Leo Scheer's boat neared the shore of Omaha Beach on Normandy Beach on June 6, 1944, it hit two mines in the water. "We were told to strip our gear and abandon ship," he said. The weight of life vests, layers of clothing and combat boots dragged many soldiers into the frigid waters. "Drowned bodies floated in those waters for weeks," said Scheer. "Many washed up against the sea wall with not a scratch on them."

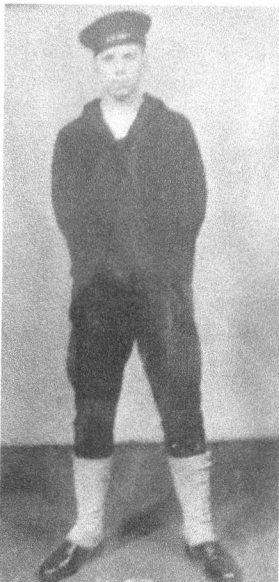

Scheer had enlisted in the U.S. Navy a few months after graduating from Huntington Catholic High School in June 1942. After completing basic training at Great Lakes Naval Training Center in Ill., Scheer was assigned to the hospital corps school. He trained at Great Lakes and at Pensacola, Fla., before being assigned to the 7th Navy Beach Battalion. "We underwent strenuous training like commandos," he said. At Fort Pierce, Fla., Scheer's squadron was attached to the Army Combat of Engineers.

Scheer's group was preparing to invade Europe for Operation Overlord, the code name for the Allies' invasion of France at Normandy. Despite months of training, nothing went according to plan. Those who made it to shore were ordered to the west end. Scheer was almost killed twice from gunfire as he crawled along. Finally, he arrived, only to find the squadron doctor missing. Wearing the Red Cross arm band and helmet, he commenced to help injured soldiers. Soldiers were treated on the sand. "We eventually got a spot in front of a house and put the casualties there," he said.

> **"I buried myself under the sand and in the morning crawled out, glad to be alive."**

A barrage of artillery forced him to administer medical attention while lying on the ground. "Even getting on your knees was risky," he said. The first course of action was to stop the bleeding. "We tried to prevent shock and used morphine when necessary," he added. "We removed medical supplies from bodies of dead soldiers because it was all we had." Bandages were packaged in waterproof tins which also contained morphine shots.

Artillery fire continued non-stop for days. "You slept fully clothed with your helmet on," said Scheer. "Shells came in close. I buried myself under the sand and in the morning crawled out, glad to be alive." Once, Scheer discovered a trio of soldiers lying on the ground. Two of the soldiers were dead. The third soldier was lying on his side, wounded by a bullet in his thigh. "It had not hit a bone but lay in the hip socket," said Scheer. Unable to move the soldier, Scheer treated him for three days, checking on him often. By the third day the soldier was moved to a landing craft. "I slept good knowing that guy had been helped," he said.

One of the worst things for Scheer occurred one night as an 88-mm cannon shot at Allied troops from a pillbox. "The Germans behind that fortification had sunk 10 of our boats," he said. "The Navy was interested in taking it out." Ten American Navy destroyers bombed the pillbox. When overspray drifted back on Scheer and other Allied troops, it killed some soldiers. "We were being shelled by enemy and allies alike," he said. Finally, an Allied battleship fired three 14-inch guns at the pillbox, disabling it.

As the Allied Army moved inland, Scheer was reassigned to the USS Lander for the Philippines, then Pearl Harbor. He also sailed to the island of Ulithi in the western Pacific Ocean and below the equator to New Guinea where he aided a ward of soldiers suffering from shell shock. He was on a ship headed back to the Philippines when news came of the dropping of the atomic bombs on Japan.

Scheer was discharged in early 1946. He returned to his job as a bricklayer, working for his family's business in Huntington until retiring.

In 1947 he married Dagmar Carlson from Chicago. Scheer joined his local VFW and became a charter member of the National World War II Museum in New Orleans. At the museum's request Scheer donated his web belt for its collection.

"I was glad I had the opportunity to serve my country during World War II," he said. "I've always loved history, and now I can say I participated in something unique. I also know I have a guardian angel that saved my life many times."

Scheer participated in Honor Flight for Northeast Indiana in May 2014.

More than seven decades after the end of World War II, Scheer continues to display a variety of photos in his room from his military life.

Millard Jacob Schwartz – Army / Europe

"I prayed every day God would let me live," said Millard Jacob Schwartz of Berne. From December 1944 through February 1945 he fought with thousands of other Allied troops against Axis troops in Belgium. The battle became known as one of World War II's most challenging, the Battle of the Bulge. "The Germans built what was called the Siegfried Line," he said. "This consisted of miles of stone cement fixtures with pillboxes behind which they hid to fire at us."

Firing guns was a far cry from the peaceful life Schwartz had experienced as a farm boy in Adams County. Born in 1921 in Berne, he completed two years at Monroe High School before quitting to help his father on their 80-acre farm.

In November 1942 he was drafted into the United States Army. Assigned to the 94th Infantry, he completed training at

Camp Phillips in Kansas, practicing with live ammunition and 105-millimeter Howitzers.

In September 1943 Schwartz traveled to Tenn. to practice war games. During a furlough home in November, he married long-time sweetheart, Betty Flesher. "We had met on a blind date two years earlier," he said. After the wedding, Schwartz reported for training at Camp McCain, Miss. The couple would not see each other again for two years.

In July 1944 Schwartz's 94th Division and 18,000 other American troops sailed from New York harbor for Europe on the Queen Elizabeth. German submarines had been sinking American ships in the ocean. For reassurance Pfc. Schwartz carried a Bible given to him by members of Gideons International. After landing first in Scotland, then England, troops moved to Utah Beach in France.

> **During the Battle of the Bulge, Schwartz and other soldiers slept in their clothing with blankets that froze to the ground.**

The battle of D-Day had begun in June but fighting continued. At one point Schwartz's division captured 60,000 German soldiers. "They were glad to be taken prisoner because it meant they didn't have to fight," he said.

Victory was not easy during the Battle of the Bulge the following winter. That area of Belgium recorded severe low temperatures and much snowfall. "We couldn't put up tents or dig foxholes because the ground was frozen," said Schwartz. He and other soldiers slept in clothing with blankets that froze to the ground.

Once Schwartz's regiment was visited by General George C. Patton. "When we stood at attention, I noticed how tall he was," said Schwartz. "I thought he was a good man."

When Axis leaders surrendered in summer 1945, not all Allied soldiers were sent home. Corp. Schwartz (he had been promoted) was one who helped maintain peace in sections of Europe and the Pacific. Schwartz's post-war duties included cleaning up the prison camp of Dachau in Germany. The horrors he saw there are still difficult for him to discuss. "Dead bodies were stacked everywhere," he said. Schwartz also visited Eagles Nest in Germany, Hitler's mountainous retreat center.

Schwartz was discharged with the rank of sergeant on January 1, 1946. Among the souvenirs he brought home from the war was a P38 pistol. "It was the type issued to German officers," he said. Other souvenirs included a Nazi flag, German Army rifle, and bayonet.

After the war, Schwartz lived in Jay County and worked for REMC. He and Betty became parents to two sons. In 1974 Millard and Betty traveled to Europe with hundreds of other World War II veterans and family members to commemorate the war. "A lot of tears were shed on that visit," he said. "I wasn't sure I wanted to go, but in the end I was glad to have attended."

In 2012 Millard Schwartz was awarded an honorary Master's degree in Military Arts from Cumberland University for his time spent with the Tennessee Maneuvers.

Of his time spent in the military during World War II, Millard Schwartz said, "I was not a hero, but I was proud to serve my country. I thank God for allowing me to come back in one piece."

Each Memorial Day the owners of Willshire Home Furnishings Store in Willshire, Ohio feature displays from dozens of military veterans, including that belonging to Millard Schwartz.

Don Shady – Army Air Corps / Europe

"I knew we had been hit when my earphones went dead," said Don Shady of Bluffton. He co-piloted a C-47 during an Allied attack against German forces over Holland. The operation was code named 'Operation Market Garden'. "We were shot by small arms fire on the ground," he said. "When your plane flies low enough to drop paratroopers, it becomes a target."

Shady was born in Allen County but grew up near Monroe. After graduating from Kirkland High School in 1942, Shady attended Indiana University as a pre-med major for one semester before enlisting in the Army Air Corps in December. Why did he want to join the newest branch of the American armed forces? "I wanted to be up in the air where it was clean," he said.

Shady was accepted into pre-flight training and sent to San Antonio Aviation Cadet Center (renamed Lackland Air Base in 1948). In ground school pilot candidates were tested on math, geography, Morse code, weather, and aircraft identification. Shady trained in a PT-19 and AT-7.

In January 1944 he graduated with class 44A and was assigned to the 78th Troop Carrier Squadron, 435th Troop Carrier Command. He advanced through primary, basic, and advanced courses at Austin and Stamford in Texas and Winfield, Kan. Weeding of pilots who could not keep up occurred at each level. "I always felt lucky to progress through each stage," he said.

After earning his aviation wings, Shady was sent to Welford Park, an American military site near Berkshire, England, 60 miles west of London. He co-piloted a C-47 plane with a crew of navigator, radio operator, engineer, and pilot. The crew's mission was to pull gliders, haul troops and freight and, if needed, drop paratroopers into occupied territory.

> *Small arms fire from ground troops pierced Shady's plane and hit the gas tank. The plane barely made it back to England.*

In September 1944 Allied air forces were called into battle in the German-occupied Netherlands. American forces were ordered to break through German lines and seize the bridges in the Netherlands. Hundreds of planes flew over the area, including Shady's C-47. Known as Operation Market Garden, it was the largest airborne operation to that time.

As Shady's plane entered the country, it flew slow and low, dropping paratroopers who would do battle on the ground. Small arms fire from ground troops was fierce. When bullets pierced Shady's plane, it hit the gas tank. The plane's steering and navigation were not affected, but the plane barely made it back to England. "The slip stream in the atmosphere kept gas in our plane until we got home," said Shady. During battle, a bullet clipped his earphone wire, bringing the enemy too close for comfort. "We were an easy target," he said. The invasion over the Netherlands was immortalized in the 1977 movie 'A Bridge Too Far.'

In December 1944 Shady, who was by now a 1st Lieutenant, was involved in another conflict -- the Siege of Bastogne. It was a battle between American and German forces at the Belgian town of that name. Weather aided the German army's efforts. "A low ceiling from cloud cover prevented us from taking in supplies early, but we flew on Christmas Day and the day after," said Shady. The siege lasted one week until the nearly depleted American forces were relieved by General George Patton's Third Army.

One happy event was when Shady's crew carried liberated Polish prisoners of war back to their homeland. "They were filthy and we had to delouse the plane after each trip, but it was rewarding," he said.

When Japan surrendered in August 1945, the war was over. Shady was discharged and returned to Indiana.

A souvenir he took with him was a 'short snorter'. This military slang refers to a string of paper money collected and taped together from places an airman had been stationed during the war. A typical added feature was signatures from the flight crew. Shady's short snorter extends 12 feet and includes money from many European countries.

After the war, Shady, who lives in Bluffton, worked at Central Soya in Decatur for 38 years before retiring. "I consider my time as an American soldier to be a good experience," he said.

Pilots aboard a U.S. Navy aircraft carrier receive last-minute instructions before taking off to attack industrial and military installations in Tokyo, February 1945.

Max Shambaugh — Army Air Corps / Europe

When a German mortar shell pierced the wing of the B-17, cutting off gas supply to the plane's engines, Max Shambaugh knew he was in trouble.

The Fort Wayne native had worked his way through two years of college at Purdue University prior to being accepted into pilot training through the Army Air Corps (the college requirement was dropped later in the war).

Shambaugh's father had been a soldier in WWI and Shambaugh wanted to serve his country as a fighter pilot. When the Japanese bombed Pearl Harbor, Shambaugh enlisted. His plans to be a fighter pilot were dashed, however, as the Army needed bomber pilots.

Attached to the 8th Air Force, 91st Bomb Group Heavy Aircraft, Shambaugh was trained to fly a B-17. "It had a 100-foot wing span, carried two and a half tons of bombs and 12 50-caliber machine guns," he said. The military nicknamed the B-17 'The Flying Fortress'. Shambaugh trained at Lockbourne Air Force Base near Columbus, Ohio, then in assimilated air battles in Pecos, Texas.

In September 1944 Shambaugh and other American troops shipped out from New Jersey to England. By the end of the fall, Shambaugh and the 10 members of his crew (co-pilot, navigator, radio operator, bombardiers, and gunners) had flown a dozen bombing missions over Germany without mishap.

That ended one night near Berlin when a shell exploded directly under the airplane. It tore through the cockpit, penetrating the steel under Shambaugh's seat. He was thankful that on the previous day he had placed steel pieces under his plane seat. "That saved me from certain death," he said.

> **The plane crashed, digging itself into the ground. Shambaugh landed against the windshield, stunned. Then he pulled out his .45 pistol and crawled out of the cockpit.**

As senior crew member of the spiraling aircraft, Shambaugh's goal was to save the others aboard. He ordered them to bail with their chutes. They quickly obeyed. Alone, Shambaugh knew he was too close to the ground to jump. Turning off the plane's electrical switches, he was tightening his seatbelt when the plane crashed. It bounced once before digging itself partially into the ground. Shambaugh landed against the windshield.

Stunned, he quickly pulled out his .45 pistol and crawled out of the cockpit window to the wing. He was prepared to engage German soldiers in a fight if necessary when he spotted his co-pilot, JD, running towards him. He was equally relieved to see peasant farmers approach.

Shambaugh quickly realized he had landed in occupied France. The farmers were part of the Resistance effort to rid their land of German troops. They quickly aided Shambaugh and JD by providing hiding places in homes. The airmen remained hidden in the homes of the French peasants for three months, despite searches. "The German soldiers would have shot us on sight if they had found us," said Shambaugh, adding that the farmers would have been punished as well.

When Shambaugh and JD eventually made it back to the American army's front line, they shocked the soldiers who were convinced the two had died in the crash. Shambaugh was happy to discover all seven of his flight crew, though wounded, had survived the crash.

Shambaugh returned to flying and during the Battle of the Bulge, he bombed bridges, factories, oil refineries and roads. By March 1945 Shambaugh had flown 35 combat missions and shot down a dozen enemy aircraft. That spring he returned to the U.S. where he ferried military planes until the war ended in August 1945.

Upon being discharged, Shambaugh continued military service with the Air Force Reserves for six years flying C-46s and AT-6s. He retired in 1951.

Using the GI Bill, Shambaugh earned a degree in mechanical engineering at Purdue University in 1947. He and his father established a construction business in Fort Wayne, which continues today with family members. Max Shambaugh retired from the business in 1992 and lived in Fort Wayne.

In 1965 Shambaugh traveled to France to find the French family who saved him after being shot down. He located the farmer and his family. "It was wonderful seeing them again and expressing my thanks for their help," he said.

When people tell Shambaugh he is a hero, he denies it. "I did what I was told to do," he said. "The real heroes were those who died in the war. Every day of my life I have felt lucky to be alive."

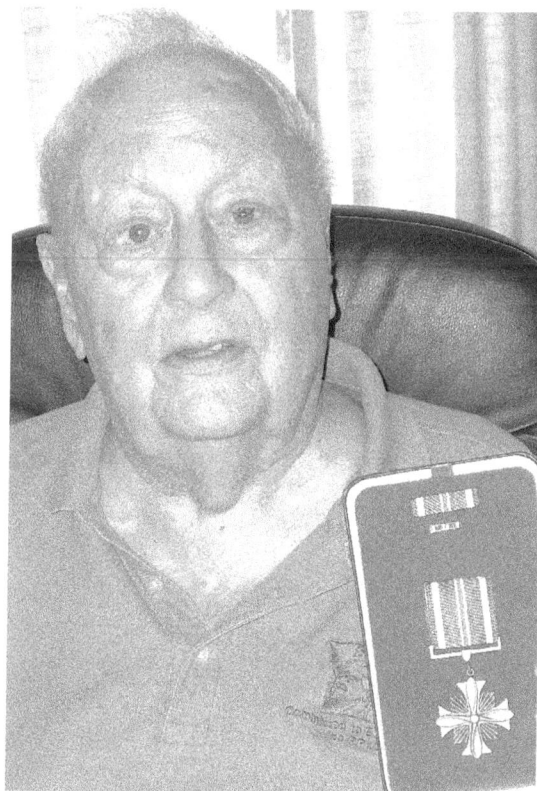

An American officer and French partisan crouch behind a car during a street
Fight in a French city, ca. 1944.

Richard Vanderwall – Navy / Pacific

"By the time our ship reached Pearl Harbor on December 12, 1941, oil from the explosions of American ships was three inches thick on the water," said Richard Vanderwall of Fort Wayne.

Vanderwall was a Seaman 2nd class assigned to the cruiser USS Indianapolis in the United States Navy. His duties included keeping the ship's log and being stationed on the bridge above two batteries of 8-inch guns. Such a position would result in permanent hearing loss in one of his ears.

The Indianapolis on its way to Johnston Island, 700 miles southwest of Honolulu when the attack occurred at Pearl Harbor on December 7. Upon hearing of the Japanese attack, the ship turned toward the island to aid where needed. The battle was nearly over, but at 1800 hours on December 12, a Japanese sub fired on the Indianapolis. Thankfully, it missed. "One of our destroyers blew him out of the water," said Vanderwall.

Born on a Potawatomi Indian Reservation in Delia, Kan., in 1921, Vanderwall graduated from high school in Soldier, Kan., in 1939. The Depression made it nearly impossible to find a job. His father had been a sailor with the U.S. Navy during World War I. He recommended Richard join the military and be guaranteed a pay check. Vanderwall passed all of his tests at the recruiting station in Topeka, and enlisted in the Navy in February 1940.

Vanderwall completed basic training at Great Lakes Training Center near Chicago (today it is called Naval Station Great Lakes) and was assigned to 120 Company G. Vanderwall was sent to Treasure Island Naval Base in San Francisco, where he was assigned to the USS Maryland. In May 1940 the crew set out for Honolulu. During the 2,200-mile trip, Vanderwall acquired his sea legs. "I was never sick," he said. He had received a New Testament Bible from his mother and read it.

At Pearl Harbor Vanderwall was transferred to the Indianapolis. By September 1942 his rank was Quartermaster 2nd Class. The American Navy, though damaged heavily by Japan's destruction at Pearl Harbor, recovered.

> *In 1943 the Allies regained control of the Aleutian island of Kiska. It would be the first and only time Japanese forces had occupied American soil during the war.*

In February 1942 on the island of New Britain at Rabaul, Japanese bombers attacked American ships, including the Indianapolis. The ships escaped damage, while shooting down Japanese planes with anti-aircraft fire, aided by fighter planes in the area.

Another naval battle for Vanderwall took place at Kiska, Alaska. The Japanese had captured Kiska, part of the Aleutian Island chain, on June 6, 1942. It was the first Japanese campaign to successfully overtake American soil. The next day the Japanese captured the nearby island of Attu.

In October the crew of the Indianapolis and other American vessels fired on the Japanese troops at Kiska. The Japanese returned fire, but Allied forces finally gained control of the island in 1943. Vanderwall and other sailors involved in the skirmish earned a battle star for the endeavor.

Danger did not always come in the form of enemy fire. In November 1942 Vanderwall's ship encountered a typhoon with 15-foot waves and winds of 100 knots

104

(115 miles per hour) that lasted for two days. "We were approaching the Unimac Pass in the Aleutian chain," said Vanderwall. "Despite bad weather, we cleared the pass and kept the ship steady."

In November 1942, Vanderwall was reassigned to the cargo ship, USS Tuluran, at Treasure Island near San Francisco. During 1944, Vanderwall was sent to Washburn University in Topeka and University of Notre Dame to enroll in courses for aeronautical engineering. At Notre Dame he met a young woman named Erma who was a hostess at the Service Men's Center. Hostesses danced and provided conversation with soldiers. Erma left the center with her date but returned to dance with Vanderwall.

The two kept in touch following Japan's surrender in August 1945. Vanderwall was discharged in February 1946. He and Erma married in April 1946.

Vanderwall used his GI ('government issue') to attend Washburn University. By the time he graduated in 1949, the Vanderwalls had become parents to two children. They would later add four more. Richard Vanderwall became an insurance salesman working in LaPorte, Muncie, Fort Wayne and Minn. Richard and Erma retired in Fort Wayne. "I am proud to have been involved as an American sailor in World War II," he said. "The experiences I had at that time have been with me all of my life."

In 2011 he participated in Honor Flight for Northeast Indiana.

A line of Coast Guard landing barges carries the first wave of invaders to the beaches of Luzon, Jan 1945

John William Wearly – Army / Europe

Bullets flew at John Wearly as he and a group of 10 Allied soldiers from Company M, 39th Infantry, 99th Division ran toward two abandoned jeeps deep in the Ardennes Forest. While fighting the German army, they had become cut off from their unit. The soldiers hoped to escape by driving away.

Unfortunately, one jeep was lodged on a tree stump. The soldiers fled on foot toward Murigen in Belgium along with members of the second division. They eventually arrived at Wirtzfeld and joined the rest of their company.

Wearly, a native of Huntington, nearly didn't make it into the military. When the war started for the U.S. in December 1941, he was deferred from active service to work in a machine shop in Huntington, making 20-millimeter anti-aircraft shells.

Upon quitting the factory a year later to attend Ball State University for a degree in education, he was drafted.

Wearly completed basic training at Camp Van Dorn at Centerville, Miss. and maneuvers in Shreveport, La., and Camp Maxie near Dallas. "We learned to shoot flame throwers, machine guns, bazookas, and Browning rifles," he said.

After Wearly and thousands of other troops left Boston Harbor for Scotland in September 1944, they crossed the English Channel to Le Havre, France, riding trucks to Wirtzfeld. The fighting that would begin there on December 16, 1944, was officially referred to as the Ardennes Offensive. Its more common name was the Battle of the Bulge.

> *When Wearly felt a bullet whiz by his right ear, he ran to his foxhole while another soldier returned fire for his cover.*

Wearly and his company walked to Elsenborn in Belgium, but the danger was not over. Nightly, Wearly, in charge of his company's radio, left his foxhole to check the phone lines. "I couldn't allow the lines to get buried in the snow," he said. "At night someone in our camp was always on the phone describing our status to HQ."

Once when Wearly felt a bullet whiz by his right ear, he fell in the snow as though struck. When an Allied soldier called out, asking if he was OK, Wearly assured him he was. He then ran to the safety of his foxhole while his friend returned fire for his cover.

Bitter temperatures of 20 below and snowfalls of four feet made fighting even more of a challenge as soldiers struggled to avoid frost bite. "We wore two pair of long johns, wool and waterproof pants, woolen shirt, sweater, mackinaw, gloves, knit cap and helmet," said Wearly. Despite frigid cold and fighting in unknown territory, the 15,000 Allied soldiers in Wearly's division were intent on conquering the Germans. "We were scared but knew what we had to do," he said.

By February 1945, the German army was defeated, but occasional bouts continued. Wearly's division crossed the Ludendorff Bridge (otherwise known as the Bridge at Remagen) on March 10. Two days later, during a gun fight, he was struck by a piece of shrapnel. It was his 23rd birthday.

Wearly recovered and during the next several months, he helped liberate thousands of Russian and Polish prisoners at Muhldorf and Moosberg work camps.

After Victory in Europe day in May 1945, Buck Sgt. Wearly, lacking the required number of points to be discharged, was assigned to teach American soldiers how to read. During the summer, now Sgt. Wearly joined the 79th Division and became supply sergeant for a camp of 1,000 German prisoners.

He joined the 102nd Division at Lichtenfels, Germany, where he taught American history to soldiers. In December 1945, after being transferred again to the 80th division at Aschaffenburg, Germany, Wearly was sent to Camp Lucky Strike. This disembarkment camp at Le Havre, France, was for soldiers awaiting return to America. On February 3, 1946, Wearly was discharged at Camp Atterbury.

After the war, Wearly earned multiple degrees in education, teaching Industrial Arts at high schools in northeast Indiana for 34 years. He then changed careers to become a director of Boy Scouts for Adams, Jay, Wells, Huntington counties.

In 1951 Wearly married Mary Jo Krick. They became parents to three children.

In 1992 Wearly's son, who was in the Air Force, and two grandsons accompanied him to Europe for the 50th anniversary of the America's involvement in WWII.

"We were all scared at different times," said Wearly. "But I was glad to serve because I had good training."

Jewish civilians become evacuees upon the destruction of the Warsaw Ghetto, Poland, 1943.

Gareth Wiedekehr – Navy / Pacific

Gareth Wiedekehr of Berne, faced death three times while serving as a sailor in the Pacific during World War II.

Upon being drafted into the U.S. Navy on August 5, 1943, Wiedekehr attended boot camp at Great Lakes Naval Station in Ill. He received training for Morse code at Northwestern University in Evanston, Ill., and graduated as a Radioman 3rd class, equivalent to a sergeant in the Army. At a Naval Station in Norfolk, Wiedekehr undertook amphibious landing training. "We were told we'd be sent to the South Pacific for invasions," he said.

Sailors traveled by train to San Diego, then on a new destroyer, the USS Cushing to Pearl Harbor. At Pearl Harbor Wiedekehr was a crew member on a landing craft. This 40-foot boat helped with invasions of Japanese-held islands in the Pacific. "We were a floating communications center for combat troops and equipment fighting on shore," he said. "Each of the 50 ships in our convoy had radios so we could keep in contact with them during battle."

Wiedekehr's ship traveled to Leyte, then Luzon in the Philippine Islands. During the invasions at these beaches, Japanese bombarded the ship with mortars. "I could hear shrapnel hitting the steel hull," he said. "I often expected a direct hit, which would have meant death for all onboard."

During the battle, Wiedekehr felt God speaking to him: "I am sparing you and all of your shipmates because your father is conducting family worship at home and praying for you at this time." Wiedekehr saw the coxswain on deck run to the bow. With a knife he cut the rope that held the ship's anchor. The engine was gunned and the ship moved out among the battleships that pounded the beach with explosives. Wiedekehr later learned the time of the ship's attack and time his family had conducted family devotions coincided.

> **"Our radar picked up two Japanese torpedo bombers. I prayed for God's protection."**

Another time when Wiedekehr's life was in danger occurred during a quiet hour while standing along the ship's rail. "I heard a buzzing noise and looked up to see a Japanese kamikaze plane flying overhead," he said. As the pilot nosedived toward the ship, the ship's gunners fired on him. "They exploded a shell in front of him and knocked him off course," said Wiedekehr. "He landed in the ocean."

On a third occasion Wiedekehr was on deck when 'general quarters' sounded. That meant all men who had assigned battle stations must report to those areas at once. "Our radar had picked up two Japanese torpedo bombers," said Wiedekehr. Knowing a strike to the ship could cause it to explode in a ball of fire, Wiedekehr again bowed his head. "Every second I thought I'd be out of this world," he said. "I prayed for God's protection."

When a U.S. plane finally shot down the enemy planes, every sailor on board cheered. "We saw those Japanese fighters nosedive into the ocean and were so relieved," he said.

Wiedekehr admired another soldier who demonstrated religious faith while serving in the military. "Jack McCurry served as a signalman with flags and was a Southern Baptist," he said. "When Jack prayed, he did so on his knees beside his bunk. No one made fun of him." McCurry survived the war and worked for the United States postal service.

The war was over in 1945, but Wiedekehr did not receive his discharge papers until April 6, 1946. Three months before he was discharged, he had written a young female friend he had known in Berne, asking if they could date when he returned home. She agreed and sent him a photo of herself. Wiedekehr and Treva Habegger married in 1947.

Wiedekehr graduated with a degree in missions from Fort Wayne Bible College. He and Treva served as missionaries in Africa with the Christian Missionary Alliance Church. They were parents to three children. "Freedom means a lot to me," said Wiedekehr. "It usually costs somebody something." Wiedekehr participated in Honor Flight for Northeast Indiana in 2011.

Japanese POWs at Guam bow their heads upon hearing Emperor Hirohito announce Japan's unconditional surrender, August 1945.

Mary Anna ('Marty') Martin Wyall -- WASP

"Being a WASP changed our thinking about everything," said Mary Anna Martin Wyall of Fort Wayne. Among the 25,000 applicants for the WASP (Women Airforce Service Pilots) during WWII, she, a native of Indianapolis, was one of 1,830 women accepted and one of only 1,074 who completed the program.

Martin learned about the WASP from a magazine ad while studying bacteriology at DePauw University. The idea of flying intrigued her. "There was a war on and I wanted to help my country," she said.

Her family was not keen on the idea. "Mother thought it was morally wrong for me to join the WASP," she said. "She came from the Victorian era. I told her she would have to accept it because if I was accepted, I planned to work hard. Dad supported me and wrote me daily."

Each WASP was required to have 35 hours of flying before joining the program. Martin paid for private flying lessons after graduating from DePauw in 1943 and while working in the serology lab at Eli Lilly.

After being accepted in May 1944, she traveled at her own expense to Avenger Air Field in Sweetwater, Texas, where the WASP trained. Since the WASP program was not recognized by Congress as part of the military, female recruits paid for their own training, uniforms, room and board. "People kept telling us we were in the military," said Martin. "Until Congress passed a bill saying we were in the military, we were not afforded benefits."

> *"Mother thought it was wrong for me to join the WASP. I told her she would have to accept it because I planned to work hard."*

Each WASP learned military protocol and procedures. They also were taught to fly a PT-17, Stearman open cockpit, BT-13 and AT-6. "The AT-6 was wonderful because it had a canopy," said Martin. "When I flew the Stearman, the wind whipped the scarf across my helmet and goggles." The training was nearly identical to what male pilots had completed, including learning to fly in inclement weather and at night. Before earning their wings, each woman completed a 2,000-mile solo cross-country flight.

Martin's class graduated December 7, 1944. Two weeks later, the program abruptly closed. "Some people believed the war would be over soon," she said. Male pilots who had flown dozens of overseas combat missions arrived home, ready to resume their flying assignments. The WASP, the nation's first group of skilled female pilots trained to fly American military aircraft, was sent home, all paying their own way.

Back in Indiana, Martin flew as a commercial pilot for businesses. In 1946 she married Eugene Wyall and they became parents to five children. The efforts of the WASP went unnoticed until 1977 when President Jimmy Carter signed a law stating they could be recognized as veterans of WWII.

In March 10, 2010, Wyall and other WASP were awarded Congressional Gold Medals for their service at the Capitol in Washington D.C. Families accepted medals on behalf of deceased WASP. At the time of the award ceremony Wyall was the only WASP still alive in Indiana.

She attended the ceremony with family, including granddaughter Hannah Wyall, a cadet at the United States Air Force Academy. Later, the Academy presented Cadet Wyall with a special pin for her uniform. "Her commanding officer told her to wear it to represent her family's military legacy," said Marty Wyall. Hannah Wyall has since graduated from the academy and been accepted into the Air Force's flight training program.

In 2010 the Indiana State Museum organized an exhibition of Wyall's military experiences. The exhibit highlighted Wyall's training and involvement as a WASP and featured her military effects and Congressional Gold Medal which she loaned to the museum. The museum also provided photos of Wyall for this book.

 "We WASP didn't care about the pay or recognition," said Wyall. "We just wanted to help our country win the war."

Jewish children, released from Buchenwald Concentration Camp, travel to new lives in Palestine, June 1945.

Paul Zurcher – Army / Europe

Buried in a foxhole on the front lines of battle in Italy in 1943, Paul Zurcher often feared for his life. "I never knew if I would survive another day," he said.

Drafted into the Army in 1943, Zurcher from Monroe, Ind., completed basic training at Camp Hood in Texas. He was scheduled for heavy artillery training in the mountains of Colorado. However, due to a high number of casualties sustained by the 10th Mountain Division in Italy, 19-year-old Zurcher was sent to that country as a replacement.

The 10th Mountain Division was a machine gun squadron with gunner, assistant gunner and ammunition bearer. Zurcher served as the ammunition bearer, marching behind the gunner. "I carried the ammo on my back and fed it to the squad when it got low," he said. It was an unenviable position as long-range artillery fire could flip over the backs of soldiers and destroy what was behind. "Our rear line stayed back because they wanted to keep out of danger," he said.

When ammo ran low, Zurcher had to retrieve more by going back for supplies. This meant running usually in the open with no protection. "When the front line moved ahead, we kept watch for enemy soldiers along both sides," he said. "If we didn't get every German in hiding, I'd be a sitting duck when I went back."

Zurcher was involved in a major conflict when his squadron received orders to take a mountain. As they crept toward the forward slope before daybreak, the squadron was uncertain of the enemy's location. Suddenly, fire pelted them on both sides and the front. Germans had surrounded the mountain and hid in pillboxes.

> *"When the front line moved ahead, we kept watch for enemy soldiers. If we didn't get every German in hiding, I'd be a sitting duck."*

The land in front of the mountain was plowed. The Allies dove between furrows for cover. "We were pinned down by the rapid fire of their 50-caliber machine guns," said Zurcher. By the time the Germans were done shelling, the trees were devoid of branches.

Extra American troops helped overrun the ridge, but the danger was not over. "We were ordered to dig foxholes," said Zurcher. "It was not unusual for Germans to do a counter attack."

While Zurcher stayed safe on the mountain ridge, the same did not occur at Po Valley. As his squad approached a quiet village, they were fired on again. Survivors scrambled to a nearby peasant's house. Made of river rock six feet high, it ensured safety from machine gun bullets, but artillery shells rained around them. Ordered to evacuate the building, Zurcher's gunner stepped into the doorway. Immediately, he was killed when dozens of bullets pierced his body.

Zurcher, next in line, quickly drew back after being hit in the right shoulder. He and other wounded were taken to a make-shift first aid station in the basement of a nearby peasant home. They remained there until medical transport took them to a military hospital in Florence. Zurcher was treated with penicillin shots every three hours. "German bullets were thought to have poison in them," he said.

Zurcher was still hospitalized on Victory in Europe (VE) Day in May 1945. Lacking sufficient points to be discharged, he was sent back to the U.S. on a 30-day delay in route. Plans were for him to go to Japan to be part of the major invasion planned there by the Allies. "None of us soldiers wanted to be involved in that," he said.

Zurcher was on a train heading from Fort Meade in Maryland to Indianapolis in early August 1945 when he learned Japan had surrendered. "That was one of the happiest days of my life," he said.

Acting Sgt. Zurcher spent the rest of his military time at Camp Carson in Colorado Springs. He was discharged in 1946.

Back in Monroe, Zurcher founded Zurcher Tire, Inc. and Best-One Tire & Service. In 1949 he married Betty Schug of Berne. They became parents to three children. In 2014 Paul Zurcher was appointed a Sagamore of the Wabash by Indiana Governor Mike Pence. Zurcher is positive about his military service. "I'm proud to have served my country," he said.

People celebrate in Times Square, New York, at the news of Japan's unconditional surrender in August 1945.

About the Author

Kayleen Reusser has interviewed hundreds of World War II, Korean, Vietnam and post-911 veterans. Her books include, *We Fought to Win: American World War II Veterans Share Their Stories; They Did It for Honor: Stories of American World War II Veterans; and We Gave Our Best: American World War II Veterans Tell Their Stories.* They are available on Amazon and other distributors. Readers are encouraged to post book reviews.

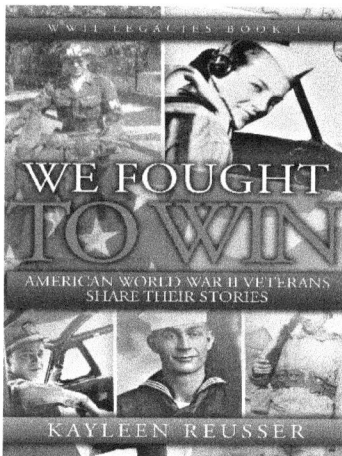

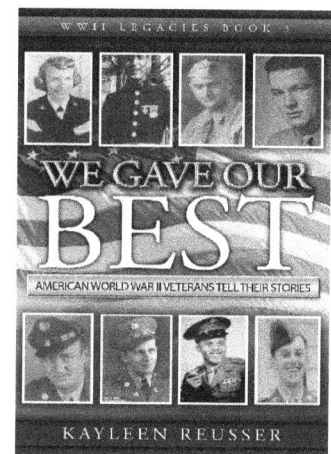

Reusser is the wife and mother of US Air Force airmen and two grown daughters. In Summer 2017 Reusser and her husband participated in a 10-day World War II tour of Europe, visiting such sites as Normandy, Remagen Bridge, Paris, Nuremberg, Bastogne, Munich, Berchtesgaden, Pegasus Bridge and other sites.

Reusser has presented talks about the trip and interviews with vets to dozens of groups. She can be contacted about speaking engagements at her website: **www.KayleenReusser.com**.

www.ingramcontent.com/pod-product-compliance
Lightning Source LLC
Chambersburg PA
CBHW081250040426

42452CB00015B/2772